# Dark Psychology

*Only 3% of People Learn How to Be a Man Who Knows How to Analyze the Psychology of Persuasion Through Manipulation Techniques and Be a Real Mind Hacker!*

**Anthony Secrets**

# Table of Contents

# Chapter 1: Introduction – What Is Dark Psychology?

# A Comprehensive Definition of Dark Psychology

Dark psychology is a term used to refer to the study of a human condition that relates to their psychological nature to victimize others. It is a common trait for all humanity to prey on fellow human beings and even other living creatures. This is usually termed as Dark Continuum. Some people are driven by this strong urge and end up being predators, while the majority suppresses it to restrain from it. Therefore, through the knowledge of dark psychology, we get to learn of these traits, beliefs, and thoughts that make a person have this behavior. From the study, we even get to know the reason why other people mistreat and victimize others for no reason as they are not after money or their belongings. Do they find it funny?

## History of Dark Psychology

There has been an array of theories trying to explain the history of dark psychology. This, therefore, makes it a target for potential misinterpretation as abnormal psychopathy. One of these theories is the dark continuum theory. Dark continuum is believed to be an imaginary line or either concentric circles that contains all the deviant, criminal, and violent behaviors. This, therefore, means that it includes the thoughts, beliefs, actions, and even perceptions that human beings experience. It is believed that dark psychology lies on the right side of the dark continuum while its manifestations lie on the left side. From this theory of Dark Continuum, we get a clear illustration depicting all forms of dark psychology, which can be termed as its origin maybe.

Another theory is the dark factor theory. This is usually termed as something that exists in all humans, which has got a direct relationship to dark psychology as from its definition. It is a theoretical equation that illustrates a person's experiences that catalyze their possibility of preying on others. It is believed from research that children from violent families always grow up to be violent. This research finding is an experience believed to contribute to the dark factor. This, therefore, shows that dark factor can be directly linked to being a contributing factor to dark psychology.

## Signs and Symptoms of Dark Psychology

Signs and symptoms of dark psychology can be categorized into two. There are those experienced by the victimizer, whereas there are those experienced by the victimized. One experiencing dark psychology can realize this through changes in attitude. This includes uncontrolled tempers, which they find themselves being violent for no reason. Another symptom of dark psychology is having violent and wayward thoughts. These thoughts are usually inclined to violence and generally victimization of others. Engaging in crime and any other related activities can also be a sign of dark psychology as one may be feeling can victimize others and easily get away with it.

On the other hand, the victim also goes through various experiences, which may indicate that they are victims of dark psychology. The signs and symptoms include having a feeling of fear, guilt, and obligation. Fear, guilt, and obligation are the major factors that make up manipulative behavior. Having fear is usually caused by being bullied or victimized, threatened, or intimidated. One will also have a feeling of guilt because they usually act to be very hurt. Another symptom that shows that you are a victim of dark psychology is always questioning yourself. Getting victimized always happens in different ways, which include how someone talks to you. If you are spoken to in a manipulative manner, it will obviously trigger wild thoughts.

## Causes of Dark Psychology

Having the signs and symptoms means that there must be a cause of the problem in question. There are various conditions that are said to be a cause of dark psychology and all other disorders involved. One of the most common causes is poor parenting. Poor parenting is in many forms, which include focusing on punishment rather than rewards. Once a child or a teenager is used for punishment, they will always think that violence is the best approach to solving problems. Having this thought will, therefore, affect their later lives a great deal and may end up being victims of dark psychology.

This problem can also be a result of the environment in which one grows. The traits of someone who grew in a home where parents live in harmony will never be the same as someone who grew up in a house full of violence. What children see as they grow up, usually referred to as their recording stage, is what they will always take it to be correct. If a child grows, seeing parents always in a fight and wrangles at home, then there is no way the child will fail to be violent too. On the other hand, the child growing up in a peaceful environment will also learn to solve issues in a peaceful way. They will, therefore, be directly affected and possibly become victims of dark psychology.

Apart from that, drugs and substance abuse is also one of the major causes of dark psychology. Using drugs to the extent that even getting addicted is a very dangerous situation one can ever be in. Hard drugs have got diverse effects on one's life, which include pre-judgment. These drugs also make them violent and always in pursuit of intimidating others. If this condition is not prevented, it may worsen and lead to even involvement in criminal activities. It might then be very hard to salvage them from the condition, thus becoming victims of dark psychology.

## Effects of Dark Psychology on a Person and Those Around Them

Dark psychology has diverse effects directly on the person and even those who are around them. These effects include indulging in social vices such as crime. Having thoughts, actions, and behaviors that are violent in nature can make one feel okay committing a crime. This has its own repercussions that may ruin their lives for good. One can be detained if he got in the act or even killed. These criminal activities also affect those around these people in that it instills fear in them. With criminal activities rising, people will not feel safe conducting their daily activities normally.

Apart from that, a person experiencing dark psychology might also cause hatred between them and others. The fact that one becomes violent and intimidates others means there is a possibility of hatred. One will be hated by those around him or her due to his or her violence and might even lead to the person becoming more violent and thus more dangerous to society. This will directly affect this person's family and those around them generally. This is because no one will feel good about being associated with someone dangerous to society. This might even worsen to make the person declared an outcast.

## Dark Psychology Probable Diagnosis. Is it treatable?

People experiencing dark psychology are always said to be going through a personality disorder and not a mental illness. There is no known cure for these people but can be controlled or rather managed. From a statement by Perpetua Neo a psychologist and therapist, she says, "From what I've read, what I've heard, what I've seen and experienced so far, people with dark triad personality disorders cannot and will not change." In reference to this statement, psychopaths can never change from their violent ways, but with the help of a therapist, they can be managed to avoid intimidating others. This does not mean they cannot go back to intimidating others but will just reduce their extent.

Apart from visiting a therapist, they can also be managed by employing reward-based treatment. Reward-based treatment entails giving people undergoing dark psychology things that they like depending on their behavior. These items can be their favorite food or even video games, among many other items. This approach can also include keeping them calm. This cannot be a cure to the condition, but it is one of the best approaches to controlling it.

## Risks Factors of Dark Psychology

There are various risk factors associated with the behaviors of persons experiencing dark psychology that if not controlled, it might cause major problems. These high-risk behaviors include criminality, violence, sexual promiscuity, gambling, and drug use. Psychopaths are usually bold and do not fear the consequences of their traits. This is because this to them is normal, and they see no wrong, and thus can be said that they have no fear of consequences.

A person with mental health disorders such as depression or anxiety is also prone to experiencing dark psychology. The mental illnesses will act as a catalyst for this condition. When a person faces discrimination from friends and even family, they may get mental disorders. This will worsen their state, and thus, it will be hard to control and manage them when they are going wrong. They will indulge in totally wrong actions without their knowledge about it. Failure to manage these problems will lead to mental disorders such as depression. This condition might worsen and lead to permanent mental illness or even death of the affected person.

Apart from that, there are other myriads of hazards that may be associated with the risk factors of dark psychology that include being jailed, abusing drugs, suicidal behaviors, gang participation, and even premature death. A person with a psychopathic condition does wrong, and to them, it is okay. This, therefore, makes them indulge in dangerous and risky activities such as abusing drugs. As a result of such acts, they might be sought out by law-keeping bodies and be judged. This will lead them to serve jail terms, which might not be good to them. Also, having a nature of violence, these persons might get to join gangs and be part of the crime. Crime is not tolerated in society and may call for serious punishment. This form of punishment can be serving a jail term and, in some cases, a death sentence.

## Avoiding Dark Psychology

Having realized that you are a victim of dark psychology, what should you do about it? Cry and whine? Dealing with this kind of manipulation as got an array of approaches. It also depends on what kind of manipulation you are experiencing. Once you realize that you are experiencing dark psychology, one should seek treatment from a qualified therapist. This will help one experiencing this that the condition is not normal and help them clear the air on that assumption.

Apart from that, one should keep boundaries which can be of great importance in mitigating the adverse effects of manipulation. Those directly facing dark psychology and find themselves always violent should always distant themselves from things that make them high tempered. This will be of great help in dealing with this abnormal situation. Manipulators always like keeping boundaries, and they hate someone being an obstruction to them. Therefore, to avoid any form of manipulation, one should just keep away from them.

## Living With People Experiencing Dark Psychology

Since this condition has no cure but can just be managed, then it means that we should devise ways to tolerate people with this condition within our societies. There are many ways of interacting with them and even making them feel better. One of the approaches is accepting their state of being violent. By avoiding the belief that all people are good and accepting the existence of bad, people will lower their expectations and give you a chance to tolerate them. Knowing that you cannot change them will allow you to understand them more and also where your vulnerabilities lie.

We can also tolerate these people by keenly paying attention to their actions and not what they say. Psychopaths are always violent and may hurl insults to intimidate you. If you focus on their words, you may get affected and worsen the situation rather than be of help. We should also try to build strong bonds and a reputation with them. This can be achieved by always being close to them and listening to what they say, even if it is wrong. This will make them listen to you and thus get an opportunity even to manage them. This will strengthen the bond and friendships, thus reducing any risks associated with the condition. It will also be a great chance to accommodate them in our societies.

# Chapter 2: Dark Triad, What Is It and Why Does It Strike?

The dark triad is a psychology term that refers to the behavioral characteristics of a person, which is, in most cases, defined with narcissism, Machiavellianism, and psychopathy. Some people rate it as a mental disorder and some as a disaster that just dawns on someone changing their behavior and how they relate to others. Dark triad generally affects a person's personality, making them take advantage of others. People with these traits tend to be manipulative, deceptive, and egoistic. They attempt to brainwash others to gain success and fame.

Politicians are, on most occasions, the worst group of people affected by this personality disorder. Their lives are full of lies, ego, and manipulation. To gain power, most of them only deceive other people to get public support and seem successful. Many people fall, victims of the dark triad, because they are not well exposed to the point of understanding what it is. They cannot easily tell when this is being used against them.

Persons with dark triad personalities have no empathy for others. They always attempt to have everything for themselves, ignoring other people's importance around them. Narcissists always want to be regarded as the most important people in society. They want to be praised and admired all the time, a kind of behavior that only manipulates others for the benefit of their own personal interests.

You may be tempted to think that these people are insane. From my perspective, to some extent they are. No one in his normal state of mind would want to have everything go their side at the expense of others. To these people that possess a Machiavellianism trait, all they always want is to win and be declared successful. They go as far as deceiving everyone around them to turn out the right person. They easily exploit the "less fortunate" in society to open their ways.

Apart from politicians, bloggers are another group of people that are overwhelmed by these traits. For example, in Kenya, we have Dr. Miguna Miguna, who is all over the social media busy manipulating people—the youth and young politicians being the most affected. He tries to make everyone his psychopath through his blogs, twits, books, and constant drama here and there.

 Can we Say Dr. Miguna Miguna is insane? He is all over seeking fame and wants everyone to believe he is always right, and the rest are wrong. He manipulates everyone, and those who follow his steps end up being disappointed at the end. Once he gets what he is looking for, he turns against you and uses your negatives to manipulate others that are not in the same line with him. He comes up with dramas to attract attention and convince everyone to believe whatever he does.

While politicians everywhere are fighting him back, the youth are becoming psychos by his blogs and keep believing that he is right because he is fighting politicians whom he claims to be the narcissists. Not to be personal, I would like to say that if you research deeply into psychology, you will find most bloggers with the same interest showing narcissism, Machiavellianism, and psychopathy traits. They won't feel guilty nor ashamed because they don't even notice that they are too much with this.

Anyone can be a victim of these traits. You may, at one point in your life, find yourself in a relationship with a narcissist, and before you notice it, you will be exploited and used by your partner. Your partner can be that antagonistic person that only feels superior to you and those around you. They will always want to be treated special and can exploit you to serve their own personal interests. They often interact in a way that shows you are less important and not as good as them.

This kind of person usually wants to be listened to. They will prefer seeking attention than empathizing with you or even recognizing your needs. Everything they do is always for their own benefit. They only concentrate on how they can feel better being in the relationship and are never ready to give you a listening year. You have no say in the decisions they make because this makes them feel less important to you and that you don't respect their decisions.

For you to know that you are in a relationship with a narcissist, you will realize that your partner doesn't really care about how you feel. They only expect you to make them happy and superior without considering what you go through for them to be what they want. Failing to meet their interests makes them feel so low and unwanted in the relationship. They make you feel like you are of no good to them and that you don't deserve them.

They can also be antisocial and low self-esteemed. They will always think of their mistakes as the worst ever and that none can be compared to them. Whenever they fail in something, they will feel like they don't fit in society anymore and that they are imperfect people. They feel so drowned and depressed as a result of one mistake.

This is always brought about by the fear of being a normal person.

On some occasions, narcissists attempt to praise themselves too much without realizing how grandiose they can be. They never stop talking about their achievements and plans in life. They always talk about how intelligent and successful they are and even exaggerate what they are capable of. They always want people to believe that their success cannot be related to someone else's. Stopping them from doing this only makes them feel stupid, and they can easily hate you for pinpointing their imperfections.

The living standards of these persons are always set high by them, which becoming realistic because they are in a way that has low standards. Their lives are usually filled with a fantasy about success, and they expect everyone around them to respect them because their destinies are thought to be successful. No one can ever change the kind of perception they have in their minds without hurting them and making them feel useless.

At some point, these people are always depressed, and no one will ever understand the reason for their depression. Understanding them becomes difficult, and if you are not a psychologist, you will always be brainwashed to serving their own interests before you notice what you are getting yourself into. You can be advised by other people, but you will not have the time to listen to what they have to say because you will have fallen a victim of narcissism, and the narcissist will, by that time have full control of you.

You are always left torn between thoughts when it reaches a point that you no longer understand a friend or a partner who has a dark personality. Failing to listen to them makes them feel worse than other people while listening to you is useless to them on the other hand. They never have time to listen to you but to seek the audience all the time.

Machiavellian leaders are the most dangerous leaders because they are always cunning and duplicitous. They always manipulate everyone from doing what they want, whether they like it or not, and they never reveal any reason for their actions. They only do that when the favor is on their side. They always make people believe that they are the most intelligent and that no one's intelligence can be compared to theirs. Those who believe in this kind of leaders are never ready to listen to other people's advice unless they are in line with the Machiavellian heads.

Dark triad strikes too much due to a number of reasons that we have discussed above and the following additional reasons.

## 1. The understanding of dark triad is not everybody's cup of tea

Not everyone has the psychology of understanding dark personality. This leads to many of us falling victims of dark triad without noticing it. We get manipulated easily and exploited to serve the interest of narcissists and Machiavellian leaders without a choice of thinking a second time or even the chance to take an alternative move. We have nothing left if not to follow their steps and support their nature of life.

## 2. The fear of standing alone

Narcissists always manipulate the big number from being on their side and supporting their ideas. This has left many people stranded between thoughts because they fear being left alone for making an opposing decision. They fear not getting a backup from those around you has led many people to fall, victims of the dark triad, since they are forced to take steps that they were not ready to take.

This usually happens with people who are often close to this kind of person or whose friends are involved with those with dark personalities. These people get convinced easily and fall into the manipulation of Machiavellian persons.

## 3. I don't want to lose a friend

Many people tend to value friendship more than their own safety. They are too much into their friend's decisions and way of life that they even forget they are also important. Such people are the most common victims of the dark triad. They easily get exploited by their friends into doing what their friends want, what makes them happy.

In this case, when you're are friends with a narcissist, then you have no choice. You will always be a tool for happiness. You will ever be ready to listen to all sorts of boasting and exaggerated stories from your friends. They will always tell you about how intelligent they are and how successful they want to become in life. The sad part of it is that nothing you say or do can ever bring a change. Your words will be meaningless to them because you have always given them room to use you.

## 4. Investing your trust in the wrong person

In many occasions, we don't always know the right person to trust. Laying your trust in someone without considering their personality opens a gate for you to be used by narcissists. This normally occurs in relationships that are just beginning, and the partners wish to travel miles away together.

Many fall into traps of their partners because they invest too much trust in them that they can never think of the negative side of them. This is what makes the narcissists overjoyed and leave them feeling so highly of themselves. They like the feeling that everyone sees the positive in them all the time and that nothing they do is ever wrong. This gives them a wide room for exploiting their partners and using them to serve their personal interests and needs. They never care about the needs of the other party, and they always want more for themselves.

## 5. Believing too fast

These narcissists always have their stories told everywhere by them and by those who believe helplessly in them. They always catch the interests of those who believe in all stories they are told because they believe the people telling the story are always right, intelligent, and successful.

The narcissist always catches the attention of others with their striking success that makes others believe in them desperately and follow their steps blindly without a third eye to see into the future and the consequences of following these people. The politicians are easily believed by their supporters, and anything used against them is like an insult to their believers. These people are brainwashed with the politicians to accept and believe in everything they do without posting questions or even having a second thought.

## 6. Most people don't care

The tendency of assuming everything said by those in authority is final is what makes us victims of manipulation and exploitation. Some of us don't even care about what is going on around them, and having no idea about it for them is even much better. Some say that something you don't know does not hurt. This is the worst mentality we have human beings. We are always there come rain come sunshine.

People with dark personalities easily exploit such people because they know the favor will always be on their side no matter what. No one will stand against them because they don't even care in the first place. What they do is right, and what they say is correct. No one bothers to know the end results of the things that they accepted ignorantly.

## 7. Psychopathy

Being too possessed with someone is what leads you to become their psychopaths. You will always want to listen to what they say, and at the end of it you will be convinced that they are right and anything said against them is wrong. You will feel pain when they are in pain are depressed when they are depressed because you have become their shadow. Whoever sees you see the person you have invested your personality in.

You are being used to serve someone's interest, and people see you like a curse to the community. Something that you never feel yourself, and you can't be told about it because nothing will ever change what you have believed in. You have invested all your thoughts in one person that you only follow what this person does or say. Every step you take towards supporting them is your best in life. Their striking success keeps you motivated that you are following the right person and that you will soon get where they are and gain as much fame as them.

Being a psycho is the worst mistake people ever make in their lives when they get possessed, not just with the right thing or person. We all need to think about our decisions and personal interests before starting to serve others who at times only need us for fame and prosperity.

Is Raila Odinga a narcissist? Does he exploit and manipulate others? Does he empathize with others or even have a listening ear? Does he ever fulfill his promises to us? This is what keeps us weighing between two people who are running for the same seat. We attempt to look into the achievements of both sides and their successful plans. We get so carried away to look for the one who best fits the seat based on the goals that each has achieved over the other.

Trying to find out what these people have achieved in their lives and starting to compare them to select the one you think can make a good leader makes us believe in the lies that are created by these people and the unseen success. We make ourselves available to be deceived and exploited with these leaders, and we end up serving their own personal needs.

We should give ourselves time to understand others before we lay our trust in them, and don't you ever forget that you are as good as the other person, and you should not be serving their interests at the expense of your own happiness.

# Chapter 3: Understanding Dark Personality and Identify It

Questionable behaviors in humans have existed for as long as humans have existed. Behaviors such as selfishness, ruthlessness, unscrupulous behavior, and evil behavior can be traced in many cultures across the world. Some of the most prominent "dark traits" associated with humans are psychopathy, Machiavellianism, and narcissism. However, many other dark traits have emerged over the years, even though some of them lack theoretical integration.

In theory, there are certain and very specific basic principles that characterize all dark traits which provide a thorough and comprehensive frame that aids in understanding dark personality. Most dark traits tend to have a specific disposition through which dark traits manifest themselves. While dark trait is downright evident in narcissism and psychopathy, it can also be seen in other classes of dark personality such as greed, sadism, egoism, amorality, and spitefulness. In this case, instead of referring to a person as being sadist, egoistic, amoral, and narcissistic psychopath, it is easier to say that the person exhibits a dark personality.

# Measuring Dark Personality

This chapter analyzes the most prominent aversive personalities. Even though these personalities are aversive, they may not necessarily become criminal or clinical. A lot of researchers have been working round the clock to understand what dark personality is and how it works. In particular, a lot of research has concentrated on examining and understanding personality traits. A lot of work still needs to be done because these personality traits still remain quite misunderstood and even understudied.

## Psychopathy

A lot of modern information on psychopathy is from the work of Cleckley in 1941. One of the most important principles that Cleckley postulated is the theory of self-control deficit, which, together with callousness, has continued to be a central concept in both criminal and non-criminal conceptions. Under extreme cases, psychopathy manifests itself through a combination of callousness and impulsivity, which culminates in a "grab and run" behavior. This "run and grab" behavior eventually turns into criminal behavior, which runs for a life-time.

In cases of self-report measures, studies on psychopathy are projected towards the non-criminal variant. People referred to as psychopaths exercise avoidance of criminal sanctions in three main ways. The first notion or assumption is that non-criminal psychopathy is less-severe compared to criminal psychopathy. The second notion is referred to as "the moderator case." Here, the theory is that when a psychopathic behavior is accompanied by attractive and socially acceptable traits such as attractiveness, intelligence, athletic ability, etc., then it is considered as being less virulent. The third notion is about people who have a psychopathic profile but only in a subset level.

## Narcissism

Narcissistic individuals are characterized by grandiose and attention-seeking behavior, which in essence is a depiction of insecurity. Psychologists believe that narcissistic behavior a 'war" between surface identity and underlying insecurity issues. This is what psychologists call 'compensatory self-promotion". The key element in narcissism is grandiose, which is defined as extremely exaggerated self-importance.

According to psychologists, the most relevant aspect of Dark Triad as far as narcissism goes is grandiose. Even though both Machiavellians and psychopaths have a common motivation called instrumental gain, ego-reinforcement is believed to the forefront motivators for these groups of people. Psychologists have, in recent years categorized grandiose variants into two categories, i.e. rivalry and self-admiration. There also exists a more ambivalent class of grandiose called *communal narcissism*. This notion holds that some section of people promotes their grandiosity by displaying superiority in a communal manner.

## Machiavellianism

Some of the prominent elements widely talked under Machiavellianism manipulation, lack of morality, and cynicism. Other elements that were added later on include reputation-building, planning, and forming coalitions. The last two qualities have been identified by psychologists as the most important in terms of identifying the constructs of Dark Triads. Machiavellians are known to plan, build strong coalitions, and strive always to keep a positive reputation. Psychopaths, on the other hand, pay very little attention to their behavior.

# Dark Personality Versus Other Models of Personality

## Normal-Range Personality and Dark Personality

One of the notable things is the overlap between clinical level PDs and normal range personality. Psychologists suggest the use of the five-factor model as the best approach to define personality dysfunction. The description is largely based on two parameters, subclinical traits, and DSM-IV constructs. These include descriptions such as paranoid, schizoid, anti-social, mischievous, and reserved, among others.

## The Big Five Phenomena and the Dark Triad

The big five models of classification were hived-off from psychological research that looked into critical elements of personality. Under this model, five dimensions have been identified. They include Openness, Conscientiousness, Extraversion, Agreeableness, and Neuroticism. Every trait under Dark Triad is thought to be negatively connected with the big five mentioned above.

## HEXACO Model Versus Dark Personality

HEXACO model is based on the discovery of a sixth dimension called "honesty-humility." This dimension entails issues relating to greed, self-entitlement, and deception. Psychologists believe that this trait is heavily connected to all the Dark triads. Negative Valence is an example of a dark trait stemming from Honesty-Humility.

## The Hogan Seven-Factor Model and Dark Personality

The Hogan Personality Inventory (HPI) is one of the variants which represent the Big five model. In this model, two traits, openness to experience, and extraversion are divided into two to represent work setting applications. Based on this, HPI was discovered to contain seven scales as follows: prudence, learning approach, ambition, sensitivity, sociability, inquisitiveness, and adjustment.

## Classification of Dark Personality Trait

While there are many studies going on about dark personality traits, there exists a big lacuna in terms of defining and classifying dark personality traits. Many available studies put emphasis on the Dark triad. While these studies shed some light on Dark Personality, they do not bring out a deep reflection of the elements and forces that drive dark personality. For example, core elements such as defense mechanisms and implicit motives are missing from these studies. It is important to take into consideration important parameters such as perceptions, motives, and abilities; all of which play a crucial role in clarifying between overt behavior and dark personality.

A good example to explain the point above is the fact that psychopathy is characterized by the inability to empathize. However, questions that can be confusing include whether psychopaths are motivated to cause harm, or they are just people who perceive the world as being hostile. On the other hand, Machiavellians are motivated by their ability to manipulate people. However, not all Machiavellians have the ability to manipulate people. This raises questions about motives and ability in regards to Machiavellians.

## Does Dark Intentions Equal Dark Outcomes?

For a long time, psychologists have grappled to answer the question of whether dark intentions in people necessarily lead to destructive outcomes. Consider the case of the classic narcissist whose motive can be easily equated to self-elevation using dominance. In this case, the narcissist clearly has a destructive intention, which is making others feel small. But does this necessarily lead to a negative outcome? Consider another person with histrionic tendencies with no intention to harm other people. However, their excessive and obsessive need for attention can be disruptive, which is a negative outcome.

From the analogy above, there are basically two ways that qualify some personality traits to be called dark, i.e., in effect, they cause and in their nature. A personality concept can be considered dark, especially if it contains malevolent characters. Such individuals may consciously or unconsciously become motivated to harm others or even themselves. It is important that a character is devoid of malevolent can equally cause noxious consequences. On the other hand, histrionic individuals do not necessarily need any motivation to control, harm, or dominate other people. However, these people may unintentionally act in a debilitating, obnoxious, and unpleasant way which may bring harm to themselves or to others.

## Understanding the Different Approaches

There exist different classifications for dark personality, which sometimes contain terminologies that are quite intelligible. For example, it sometimes becomes quite difficult to know when taxonomies refer to the same thing or different concepts. On the one hand, there is Dark Triad and HDS, which are generally quite known. On the other hand, there is what psychologists call aberrant personality, maladaptive personality, and dysfunctional personality, which falls under the six-dimensional approach. Out of these approaches, the Dark triad perspective is the most known in both organizational research and personality psychology disciplines.

While Dark Triad is the most popular approach to discussing and analyzing dark personalities, the focus must not end here. Other approaches must also be incorporated because the biggest weakness of Dark Triad is that it leaves out important elements in the subclinical arena. In any case, Dark Triad was never intended as a method for identifying and classifying dark traits.

## Dark Personality and DSM

DSM 5 is a recent breakthrough that offers immense potential for understanding dark personalities deeply. Until quite recently, clinical studies of PDs rode on the assumption that PDs were categorical. However, new evidence from DSM-5 proves that PDs take a dimensional course as opposed to a categorical dimension. Previous studies using the categorical dimension produced measurements with high comorbidity and little reliability.

Psychologists are using the new DSM-5 to classify and restructure PDs into certain core domains. These domains include psychoticism, negative affectivity, disinhibition, detachment, ad antagonism. These domains are further divided into many other facet traits, such as impulsivity, hostility, and suspiciousness, among others, which are considered to be empirically distinct in nature. Already, a number of on-going research works have started to make a comparison between the new DSM-5 model with a dark personality.

## Psychological Unconscious Versus Dark Traits

Scientists have already proven that dark personality has an element of unconsciousness. Explicit examples of these include the implicit motive for power and the implicit motive for to aggress. Based on these findings, it is important to consider the critical role of dark intentions together with other important frameworks of taxonomy, such as DSM/HDS. Further studies by scientists have revealed that traits, whether dark or bright do serve as an avenue for which implicit motives are expressed.

Today, there is a big consensus relating to the structure of bright traits (the Big Five). Dark traits, on the other side, still contain a lot of disagreements that need to be ironed out. For example, one of the areas in which consensus is yet to be reached is the issue of psychological unconsciousness. However, a number of researchers have started working on dark traits in order to bring out a better understanding of the issue of motives and unconscious process, which is thought to influence dark personality.

**What is Known**

Recent empirical studies by reputable scientists show that narcissists tend to have the highest degree of enhancement of the self-followed closely by psychopaths. Machiavellians, on the other hand, did not exhibit a significant degree of self-enhancement. These recent findings can be seen to be consistent with early evidence that Machiavellians put more emphasis on their sense of sense, whereas narcissists depict strong elements of deception in their personality.

Equally intriguing is the finding by researchers about the performance marker of psychopathy being relatively low verbal in comparison to non-verbal intelligence. The issue that has baffled many psychologists is why dark traits contain stronger non-verbal skills rather than verbal skills. One of the possibilities for this, as thought by researchers, is that frustrations that come about from an individual's inability to express and communicate their ideas could eventuate into one of the many personality syndromes. Another possibility being considered is the issue of "neurological deficits" in both Machiavellians and psychopaths.

Researchers have also found out that another way to understand dark personality is by comparison of constructs to establish their positions in the Five-factor model. Narcissistic and psychopathy tendencies have been found to be associated with characteristics such as openness and extraversion. Conversely, Machiavellianism and psychopathy have been found to be negatively connected with conscientiousness, which is known to be a communal trait. Only psychopaths have been found to be low on neuroticism, a finding which is somewhat consistent with the traditional belief that psychopaths lack anxiety.

## Traits Associated With Dark Personality

Years of research studies by different groups have come up with a consensus about a number of traits considered to result in a dark personality. Among these traits are egoism, moral disengagement, narcissism, Machiavellianism, spitefulness, psychological entitlement, self-interest, psychopathy, and sadism. People who are said to have a high degree of dark personality are believed to maximize their personal utilities at the expense of other people.

The utility can be better understood in terms of the extent of the goals to be achieved, which encompasses gains which more or less are visible. Such gains include psychological fulfillment, joy, money, status, pleasure, and power. For this reason, individuals with strong dark personalities are known to pursue behaviors that only benefit them at the expense of other people. In the extreme, these people are known to derive pleasure from inflicting disutility on others, for example, pain. It has also been revealed by researchers that people with a high degree of dark personality have no or little interest in other people's utility. A good example is being happy for other people.

Studies also reveal that people with high levels of dark personality hold dearly beliefs that justify their corresponding actions. A good example is maintaining a positive self-image even though a person clearly has malevolent behavior. There are many beliefs that are used as justification by people with dark personality, for example, the feeling of being more superior to other people, endorsing and supporting ideologies that favor dominance, adopting a cynical view of the world and considering the world to be a ruthless and competitive place among other beliefs.

While there is enough information regarding dark personality, there are still some dark areas about the matter which requires further probing in order to be fully understood. One such area is the issue of explicit personality, which constitutes the analysis of mental representations of motives and behavior that relate to introspection. Another area that requires considerable probing is implicit personality, which by nature does not operate inside conscious awareness. For this reason, it is difficult for researchers to only rely on direct assessment methods. There is a need to go deeper by also entirely using indirect methods to expose deep issues surrounding implicit personality.

Many people often wonder how to identify a person with a dark personality. One of the ways to identify such people includes a tendency to manipulate other people for someone's own gain. In addition, such people may exhibit behaviors that can be perceived as lacking in morals. These kinds of people often do not feel any remorse at all after doing something hurtful. They may even follow their thoughtless actions with callous remarks. Another trait that is considered as a standout trait in people with dark personality is boastfulness. They often brag about themselves and find it difficult to accept the fact that someone is ahead of them. Another common trait found in people with a high level of dark personality is cynicism, which is a completely distorted and jaded view of the world. This distorted view of the world helps them to progress their cause.

# Chapter 4: The Approach to Use to Talk to a Dark Personality

Some personalities will hurt you from time to time, and there is a need to know how to handle such a nature. You will meet with such kinds of people, and if you do not take precautions, you can easily give up on people. They tend to be unpleasant and are as well arrogant, and they can go to the extent of being violent. Nevertheless, there is no need to avoid a person with a dark trait since they are all over in society. Using the right approach to handle them will do more good than harm, and harmony achieved. Embracing such kind of a person and understanding them may be all they need from you to change into a better person.

The dark traits may include:

## Narcissism

Such a person is bound to have an extreme feeling of self-admiration at your own expense. They prove to be selfish, egocentric, as well as the craving for the spotlight. The intensity varies from one person to the other. A problem comes in when such a person fails to consider what the person next to them feel. The trait can go to an extreme condition, and it ends up being a mental illness.

## Machiavellianism

A person with such a character lacks empathy, manipulates others, deceit, and is a self-centered person. They are only concerned about what they will gain personally and does not respect the interest of others.

## Psychopathy

It is a character that lacks empathy, has a manipulative behavior, and is associated with anti-social tendencies. They will manipulate you for their gains. They make pleasant first impressions, and you can fail to realize their character immediately. The figure, at times can fail to affect them directly but harm the person close to them. They are never anxious about the next person's opinion, and they like to show off to strangers as a way of playing cool. They are known as being morally bankrupt since they will not find it difficult to lie to you.

## Everyday Sadist

A person with this kind of character is stubborn and enjoy being cruel to the people around them.

A person with a dark character has high self-esteem and is very sensitive when it comes to criticism. Despite that, they are the people that we interact with them daily, and we cannot avoid them no matter what. There are some great ways to help you deal and put up with them without much trouble. They include;

## Set Boundaries

A person with a dark personality always thinks that they have the freedom to express how they feel, even when it is not time for them to show. They are quick to give unsolicited advice and then end up taking credit for what you have done. They can go to the extent of forcing you to talk about your private affairs, which may not be in order. They have no sense that you need your personal space. It is then advisable for you to put clear boundaries to where and where not to get. At times, they may even not seem to recognize the set limits, and hence, there is a need for you to define them clearly. They do not care about the outcomes of crossing your boundaries since they will not suffer the consequences. It is so because they are known to pay attention to the things affecting them directly.

## Sort for a Support System

There are no chances to avoid having a conversation, such as a person. And for that, there is a need for you to maintain a good relationship with other persons who can help you deal with such kind of a personality. Knowing the type of person you are dealing with will help you get the proper support. Some will undercut and get into your way in an approach that you may not realize quickly. Some are a bit easy to get on board, while others will give you the hardest time ever. You can as well seek some professional help on how to handle such a person. Someone with a dark personality may even at times indulge in substance abuse. Often, such a person may be challenging to get into terms with them, and they need to have counseling sessions regularly. It is not their responsibility to go out there to look for help, but rather' sit's your responsibility to make sure they get help. They may be less concerned and may not know that they need help. They think everything is running the way it is supposed to be. Sorting for some help is vital because some cases can drain your mental as well as physical health. Do not do it alone, but you can involve friends and family to make work easier.

## Don't Let a Person of Dark Personality Detect the Emotional State You Are In

Letting them know your emotional state will give them away to hurt you the more. They will have the confidence to control you in any way they feel. If they can monitor your emotional state, that means they will have full control over you. Even though whatever such a person says, do not show them that it has crushed you. When they know they have hurt you, they will find more pressure to annoy you. Do not fall for their trick, no matter how nice they may seem to you. You need to know that it is a strategy that they may use to access your emotional status. Their niceness may make you think that they are a changed person while their only aim is to make you open up. Do not open up despite what because they are not sincere while being kind to you.

## Make Thing Clear To Them That What They Feel Is Not the Same Thing You Think

Making it known to them that what they believe is not your feeling might make a person with a dark character annoyed. It will be of great importance for them to know that there are no similarities between both of your emotions. You can even find words that will make them know that you understand what they feel, but you don't have the same feeling.

## Do not be Naïve

It is advisable never to trust someone with a dark trait. They do not mind hurting you, and they will never change no matter what. Do not play an innocent person, instead stick to what is right. They are extremely convincing and do not make a mistake to fall into their trap no matter what. They have good behavior that can make you fall for them quickly, but that should not fool you. It is a plan to bring you down and control you. They do this to benefit themselves at your own expense, and they end up messing with you. Do not let the person know that what they have said has pinned you down even though it might have. They should know that what they do does not affect you. Keep in mind that such people do not have the patience to listen to very long statements. The shorter and concise you keep your comments, the better for you all. They can ignore you simply because they do care whether you will be hurt or not. Confidence is crucial and does not disrespect them no matter what. Give them a chance to express themselves to make things run smooth. When you are assuming that they have no right to express their thoughts, it will mean that things will be no better. Your innocence may not be of much importance when it comes to dealing with such a character.

## Keep away from the Toxicity

When you avoid problems as well as stressful situations, you will land into them. When you avoid anxiety, you tend to make anxiety worse. Do not get close to an environment where you will feel uncomfortable. Try as much as you can to manage yourself when around a person of such character. Spend most of your time doing what you like most and avoid anything that will be of harm to you. Carefully make choices and do not expose yourself to dangers while trying to fix a relationship with such a person. Such a person will never at any given time admit they have made a mistake or even take responsibility. They will direct their negative character to you or the person next to them. In such a case, do not accept the blame since that will only feed their ego. And it is the strategy that they use to belittle you despite you may think it is a way of maintaining peace. Do not suppress the truth since that is the only way to make things straight. Be calm when dealing with a person of a disagreeable character and do not respond to anger in anger. Do not get into an argument instead of practicing calmness to avoid getting the situation more complicated. Do not be defensive and do not show them that whatever they are saying is draining you. The other party may soak in emotions, and defending yourself may even make it tighter. Try not to take the entire thing personally, and it will save you from a lot of injuries. If you get yourself in the emotional heat, take some deep breaths, and that will help you cool down.

## Change your Perception of how you view their Behavior

It will be vital if you consider their behavior from the view of strength overuse as well as underuse. It will have a vital role in how you v the person. The approach may not be productive when it comes to that person who their dark character is deep-rooted. Such kind of person may use their character strength to manipulate and harm others intentionally. Be creative on how to end a conversation and practice perseverance when dealing with a person of a dark trait. Use the qualities you pose to deal with the situation in the best way possible. Make use of your strength to cope while interacting with such a person. Take good care of your feelings using your power and forgetting your weaknesses. You can hardly control a person of a dark character, but you can manage and change yourself. Try and understand the person in the situation because that is what matters most. Try and get into their shoes, but do not give them the power to explore your feelings. Showing them how vulnerable you are will mean feeding their defenses. A person of a dark personality hates vulnerability as well as anyone trying to show its signs. You will bring down their status if you show a sign of being vulnerable. It can make them mock you as well as give them the courage to change the attention to your mistakes. Changing the way such a person operates, though legitimate, may not be fruitful. They view that as a threat to their lives. They are less concerned about want to implement a change and why should things operate differently. Have a positive view of how they do things, and that will make it easier to handle difficult situations. They can belittle you, and you do have to take that negatively way. Regardless, do not fall into it because they will do that the more when they realize you have been affected. Being positive is vital to help not utter your mind-set, and that will not affect your response towards that person with a bad character.

## Own Your Annoyance

Some people having a dark character have proved to be annoying and can get on your nerves with no regret. You can put in some effort to see to it that something happens. But there comes a time when one person interrupts the entire process. They try all their best so that they can take all the credit, and they have not contributed in any way. Without a doubt, you will not have the patience to handle such a character. But analyzing where the frustrations are coming from will help you put a stop the cause of the failures. Someone with a dark trait will use any means possible to appreciate themselves. It makes them sneaky as well as undercutting. It is useful if you understand from their point of view. All that occurs as a result of them feeling insecure, and you need to assure them. Help them settle down as well as concentrate on the exact thing that should be done for them to think once lore secure. Again, you do not have to give them much reassurance since that will fuel their egocentric. The needed amount of reassurance will make then settle and deal with the issues at hand in the right manner.

# Work With Immediate Action and Not Promises

When with a person of a dark character, do not give them a room to make promises. Insist on them taking a direct action instead because making promises is an approach many use to get their way out. Making a promise does not mean that they will deliver in most cases; they do not honor the obligations they make. Some commitments to do something, but they do the opposite of what you expect. They promise to do better, but instead, they do the things that you hate. Ask for the exact thing that you want and do not change your stand. You can insist that you will deliver once they have honored their promise. Do not compromise, and you need to be consistent so that they know you are serious about it.

## Assess the Context

Be concerned and find out some situations first before you get into a talk with a person of a dark personality. A person may have a bad character because of the hard times they are going through. Some situations can make the person's character to gain more strength and worsen if not dealt with in time. It would be best because you will know how to get into an interaction with such a person. Some people may not be wrong, but the environment they are in makes them have a bad character. Being able to distinguish between the one behaving in response to certain things will make you know how to deal with them. You handle people differently according to the cause of their character. Some tend to develop resentment that gives birth to such kind of nature even though they may not own it before. Dark traits spring a way of expressing anger, frustration, as well as sadness. Knowing the reason behind a particular character trait will help you see the approach to use to get to the person. Judging the other person and you do not know what they are passing through is probably the worst thing you will do. Someone may act unreasonably out of feeling vulnerable or expressing fear. First, pay attention to what they have to say before judging them. From there, you can know the basis to use to handle them. Let them feel acknowledged, and they will cooperate, and you will see whether it is a character they have acquired or is in them. Pay attention to what they have to say and not what they will say next. You have to be flexible for you to answer all the questions that might come up and with different answers.

## Do Not Get Emotional

When having an interaction with a person of a dark trait, make sure you do not understand emotions in the talk. Choose the best way to respond to everything rather than reacting immediately. When you are triggered, take some time to think about how to respond. Self-control is the crucial thing in such a situation since a lack of self-control will make you react in a way that will show you are a failure. It is good to know that your reactions will determine whether the person will take control over you or not. They might stir you as a tactic to test how emotional you are, and you need to have effective strategies at hand for how to or not to respond.

## Do Not Take Things Personally

When you are handling a negative person, do not take anything personality. Weigh everything they say, but do not put that in your heart. It may ruin tour emotional as well as physical health. Do not take in the excessive emotions from the negative person. When you take it personally, you are likely to react instead of acting. You may act to a negative person who is responding to how nature is treating them. Help someone have positive feelings, and you will know whether they are demonstrating by behaving in the wrong way. You may end up helping someone in the process who was undergoing difficult situations. When they do something the right way, it is good to make a compliment as a way of appreciation. Appreciating someone for something well done can make them change their behavior and embrace positivity. Reality will maintain a good relationship regardless of the character trait of a person. Detach your emotions from a conversation that you know will end up hurting you. Showing extreme emotions, for example, crying will stimulate a person with a dark character to provoke you more. When such a person reacts vigorously, do not become emotional, and join them in responding.

Treat some situations with a difference to shield yourself from unnecessary emotional feelings. Try to redirect some interactions to something a bit positive. Anything you utter while angry can cause harm and will only make the person more negative and never appreciate the positive side of people. Avoid getting in a disagreement with a person of a dark trait. Arguing will only raise the temperatures and bear in mind that the other party cares less. If a negative person proves to be difficult, try, and find a way to end the talk. Confidence will play a significant role, no matter what kind of person you are interacting with.

# Chapter 5: Mysterious Case Studies on Dark Psychology

The mystery of dark psychology has baffled many and continues to be an element of shock and wonder. It is without a doubt this kind of depraved, twisted psychology that is the driving force behind serial killers and many baffling cases that defy the human conscience. That leaves us with a question - is the dark psychology a rare occurrence in some people or we all susceptible to its depraved logic? That's a question for another day, though.

Below we look at some baffling cases that have prominently put to the fore the mystery of dark psychology. What we notice is that the worst of human traits, the darkness that lives in all of us, come out during experiments. And not just in the subjects. Even the ones experimenting showed great inhumanity.

## Scientific Experiments

The scientist has conducted experiments on people for as long as science and experiments and hypotheses have existed. Yet, there was a strange twist. It was a twist, perhaps more twisted than the entire subversiveness of dark psychology. Scientists have also been in the fore in proving the dark psychology as they attempted to find out about something else. So traumatizing were these experiments that some of the participants' permanent psychological issues. Most of them involved manipulating test subjects to get them to perform, which you will realize as one of the dark personality traits - Machiavellian.

In the 1960s, a doctor came to light after it emerged that she used electroshock therapy on children. The horror didn't start there, as, during the interview process, she would select her patients by having a parent bring their child, where she would press their heads. Any slight movement and she would declare the child was suffering from schizophrenia. And during the shock, she never showed sympathy on the children, with her youngest being just three years.

Then, from 53-73, the government of the US embarked on experiments that would help them find out how to manipulate people. The project was called MKUltra. These experiments involved subjecting people without their knowledge, to drugs that altered their brains, hypnosis, sexual abuse, and many other forms of torture. This experiment just gave a glimpse of the murk that was human psychology. Subjecting innocent people to such cruelty in the name of the research was itself peak dark psychology.

The most famous experiment in psychology was the Stanford Experiment, which aimed to find out the cause of conflict between the prisoners and their guards. The scientist selected twenty-four prisoners and assigned them roles of either guards or prisoners. Then they were awarded a model prison within the premises. What emerged was that the prisoners playing guards were so strict and so extreme in their torture of the prisoners that the scientists stopped the experiment after just six days! Sick.

The Milgram experiment was also another that put to the fore the repressed terrible recesses of human psychology. In 1961, Stanley Milgram, a Yale University Psychologist, set out to find just why Eichmann and other millions of soldiers in the Holocaust just followed orders. This was a quarter a year after Eichmann had gone to trial. Two people were placed in separate rooms but could hear each other. The experiment was to see the willingness of someone to follow authority orders. Between these two participants, one was an actor. The test subject would then read the question to the actor, and if the actor answered any of them wrongly, the test subject would administer an electric shock to the actor. Nearly every single test subject continued pressing the electric shock button when the experimenter to them that they would not be held personally responsible for their actions.

Another case was of David Peter Reimer, who was born biologically male. When he was just seven months, he suffered a damaging injury to his manhood as someone circumcised him. John Money, a psychologist and a great believer in gender as something that one learns, convinced David's parents that their son would more likely be more functional as a girl. He must have been a Machiavellian. But while Money put his money on his idea is a success, David's account much contradicted Money's. David never identified as female, so that is where it all falls apart. David spent his childhood traumatized due to being teased and ostracized, leaving him depressed. Then, at just 38 years old, David couldn't take it anymore and committed suicide with a gunshot to the head.

Another example of the scientists being total monsters was in the Washington and Oregon prison testicle radiation experiment. Between 1963 and 1973, several inmates from these two prisons volunteered as test subjects in a trial that aimed to find the effects of radiation on testicles. One hundred thirty inmates were bribed with cash and promise of parole to take part in the experiment. Here, we see the dark part of the scientist come out. Manipulating prisoners into taking part in a dangerous operation is inhumane. The inmates agreed to take part in the experiment. The study apparently was the brainchild of the government.

The scientists exposed some of the test subjects to massive doses of radiation. Now, exposure to radiation is dangerous, even when it is in small doses. Radiation rays have a permanent effect on the human cells, mutating the DNA and other cells in the body, leading to deformities. This affects not just the test subject, but the children will have as well. It was only much later that the prisoners found out that they had not been told about the whole truth regarding the dangers of the experiment. They settled a $2.4 million agreement at the turn of the century.


## Psychopaths - Serial Killers

Serial killers have, for a long time, held the fascination of many people. Their wanton disregard for necessary human conscience has forever baffled and intrigued not just the ordinary people, but the figures of authority, scientists, and psychologists.

One of the many questions that one finds themselves asking when watching a serial killer documentary is - are we responsible beings, or would we become them if we felt like we would not be held to book? If we had nothing to lose, would we be just as lethal? If the Milgram experiment above was anything to go by, perhaps we could be just as prone to violence as serial killers. But still, the lack of inhibition shown by these killers is legendary, a revelation of the darkness rolling just beneath our human conscience.

Ed Gein was a farmer in Plainfield, Wisconsin, notorious for robbing women's bodies from graves. He also was a murderer and often used parts of the women's remains to decorate his isolated farm in Wisconsin and make items on clothing. Gein was active between 1945-1957 and died in 1984 at a mental institution. He had so much impact that he was loosely used to create fictional killers.

## Night Stalker

Richard Ramirez was a deranged murderer that came to be dubbed by the media as 'The Night Stalker.' In 14 months, Ramirez embraced the night as his accomplice, gravitating towards the embrace of the dark as he made way through homes in a prowl that saw him leave behind 13 dead across California.

Before he made his first kill, the authority had arrested Ramirez for attempted rape, but the woman did not pursue the case, choosing not to testify against him. Let, free, Ramirez began a long murder spree that was violent, brutal, and callous. He often showed no remorse, and his first murder victim, 76-year old Jennie Vincow, on June 28th, 1984. Ramirez brutally raped then murdered the woman by slitting the throat so deep that she was almost decapitated.

During his trial, he gave little away in terms of remorse, and as he was led to prison to serve his life sentence. On his way to prison, he couldn't help but taunt the people gathered outside the court to witness his trial.

Ramirez had a difficult childhood, suffering two severe head injuries that left him suffering from frequent epileptic attacks. His father was abusive to him, leading to Ramirez running away from home. He found comfort in his cousin Miguel, a war veteran, who had developed a taste for torturing women in Vietnam. He showed Ramirez the photos of the torture and killed his wife as Ramirez watched. Miguel may have influenced Ramirez to develop a taste for blood.

## Grim Sleeper

When women began disappearing at a neighborhood in Los Angeles, no one would have suspected the personable Loonie Frankline Jr. Neighbors and friends described him as someone willing to help and didn't display the usual traits of psychopathy, like being a loner.

Franklin earned his nickname due to the 14-year break he seemed to have taken between murdering his first eight victims between 1985-1988. He began again in 2002, though authorities believe that he may be responsible for more deaths than the eleven the court found him guilty of.

Franklin targeted women and with hundreds of polaroid photos of women, some of whom were his victims, others who were still alive. Others were never identified, which led authorities to suspect him of more deaths than what he was charged with.

Franklin shot his victims at close range and dumped them near trash cans and on alleyways. Often, he would target vulnerable women off the streets.

He was sentenced to death in August 2016, although authorities are still trying to connect him to 15 other killings.

## Edmund Kemper

Kemper was a bright child who suffered a lot of abuse, physical and emotional, under his mother. He had also been displaying psychopathic tendencies as a child, often torturing and killing animals, which is observed in a big number of people who end up being psychotic killers.

He often decapitated his sister's dolls as a child and had once stalked his teacher in second grade outside her home with his father's bayonet. When he was ten, Kemper killed the family's cat. Then, he killed another when he was 13. This second time, he took up some parts of the animal and kept them in the cloth closet, where his mother came across them, much to her horror probably.

When he was 14, he left home to find his father in California. His determination to find his old man paid off, but rather than find comfort, the man rejected him. He had been constantly belittled by Kemper's mother, and this may have led him to hate the boy. Dejected and angry, he went to live with his grandparents, both of whom he shot dead in 1964, at just 15. He was then committed to Atascadero State Hospital for the criminally insane but was released back to his mother five years later, much to his chagrin.

He began fantasizing about killing his mother but decided first to perfect his murder skills.

Between 1972 and 1973, Kemper began his killing spree. Targeting female students, he would pick up those hitchhiking a ride on the road. But then, rather than take them to their destination, he took them out in the wild, where he killed them. Then, to further add to his derangement, he would have sex with the dead women, decapitate them and take their heads back to his apartment, where he would have sex with them too. Scary stuff this one.

Then, in 1973, on Good Friday, Kemper achieved what may have been his biggest goal—he murdered his mother. Taking a hammer, he bludgeoned her to death, then proceeded to strangle her friend. Afterward, he also defiled his mother's head.

After he was done, he made a phone call to the local police, where he confessed to them. They were initially reluctant to arrest him, as he was known to them, but they were down on him soon after he began revealing details of the murders that only the murderer would know. At this point, when they came to take him, he did not resist. He was just twenty-four at the time.

## Alton Coleman and Debra Brown

The Bonnie and Clyde of the serial killer's horrific world, the two traversed across six states, leaving eight people dead in their wake.

At age 19, Coleman had already had six counts of rape charged against him. It was reported that Coleman had unusually strong sexual urges that he then took to satisfying with all people, including children.

In May 1984, he befriended Juanita White, a single mother of two children, 14-year old Vernita White, and her younger brother. After befriending Juanita over a few weeks, he then asked for permission from Juanita to have Vernita accompany him to his house to pick up a stereo system on May 29th. Both never came back, and Vernita was found brutally murdered, raped, and bound with a TV cord.

Then, in the company of Debra, his girlfriend, they abducted two children, Tamika, and Annie as they walked and left school for home. The two were very young, seven and nine respectively. The two depraved beings then tied up the children, and when Tamika couldn't stop crying, Debra covered her mouth while Coleman, without remorse, stepped on her chest. But they were not done. They killed her by strangulation, then both defiled Annie, beat her and choked her, but Annie lived through the ordeal.

Then, on the same day, they abducted Donna Williams, from Indiana, who had known Coleman for a few weeks. She was found on July 11th, 1984. She had been strangled, and her car was close by. What this even scarier was that the incident took place just a short distance from Coleman's grandma's house.

Then, they were in Ohio four days later, where they gained the trust of another African American family, headed by Virginia Temple. Temple had three children, with Rachelle, 9, being the oldest. The pair strangled Virginia and Rachelle and then put their bodies in the crawlspace in the home's basement. The other two children were not harmed, and Virginia's mother found them when she came to visit.

Theirs was also merely a murder seemingly for the thrill of it, an indictment into the twist of human psychology when you dig deep.

According to Del Paulhus, a personality psychologist, the four dark personalities covered in chapter 3 - Machiavellian, Narcissism, Psychopathy and Sadism, these personalities are fascinating than the typical personality types, which could explain our obsession with serial killers and their actions of extreme, often without any apparent motive.

Del Paulhus called for more linking between these dark personalities typed, despite their distinct concepts.

Looking at it, you get the sense that, indeed, they are part of the same basic structure. All four personality types often will be reflective of the doers' view of the world. To kill, you will need a set of distinguishing traits, after all, to begin to murder, then keep murdering, and with increasing violence and seeming glee.

On their own, these cases of call for us to give more attention to what precisely the dark psychology is and how we can look into it further. Beneath our human conscience, lies a dark underworld, waiting for just the right trigger to come to the fore.

# Chapter 6: Incredible Historical and Political Revelations about Dark Psychology – How do They Control Us?

History is full of fascinating and incredible instances of people in authority seeking to have complete control of the people they rule.

As seen in chapter five, various governments funded experiments that were aimed to help them identify ways in which they could manipulate the human mind for better control.

But it's not just governments that manipulate us. When you look around you, consumerism is often fed down to us as the key to happiness, as the ultimate guide to how to live your life. So what is this?

## Advertisements

When Beech-Nut Packing Company hired Edward Bernays, whom we know today as the father of public relations, they expected him to do his job well as any co-operate would, but what they didn't expect was how he would change how the average American consumes breakfast. Bernays researched how Americans took their breakfast and found that many American's treated themselves to light breakfast. An internal doctor in the company suggested that a heavier breakfast would be healthier. Bernays had approached him with the question of whether a hearty breakfast would be healthier than a non-hearty breakfast. To which the doctor agreed. After posing a question about bacon being a hearty breakfast, the doctor agreed, and Bernays got what he needed.

Armed with that, he went on and created an advertisement that said that doctors recommended eating bacon for breakfast for a healthier life. And with that simple line, he manipulated the audience into eating bacon such, bacon sales, which up until that point were on a decline, went up against owing to this simple trick.

Sigmund Freud, the psychoanalyst who has become so influential in modern psychology despite his controversial hypotheses, divided the mind into three components: the conscious, the preconscious, and then subconscious. In it, his analysis of the unconscious mind is what continues to influence modern psychology. Freud believed that we kept things that we were consciously unaware of while in the conscious state of mind, although they did reveal themselves in dreams and in what is known as a "Freudian slip."

Freud believed that we kept many of our true intentions, desires, and emotions repressed because they were too threatening and that they revealed through the Freudian slip.

Advertisers then, will often take keen note of this and use it when they want to create a commercial to sell a particular product.

Because advertisers know that we desire things that we don't have at the moment we exist, they create an advertisement about a product that line with what you feel you need for a better life, to make you desire it, and want to have it in your life.

Often playing on our inability to tell weak and strong arguments about things we have poor knowledge about but which a necessary (if I don't have car engine knowledge, for example, I will choose the one where the advertisers managed to convince me that it was better, even if in reality it is no better than the competition), which is why many major adverts will be found in passive media like television, radio or magazines. In these media, you are a passive consumer; as such, you are not in the state of mind to think critically and weigh the pros and cons, the truths, and the manipulations of those truths to sell you the product.

When you watch movies or music videos, one of the techniques that many smart directors and advertisers use is the product placement technique. Unlike traditional advertising, where the whole video centers on telling you how incredible the product is, movies and music videos play on your idolization of celebrities to manipulate us into buying their product.

Product placement then, will have a character in the movie, or if it's a music video, have the artiste hold the product in a subtle, yet obvious manner that will allow you to see the product, but not create a direct link at the moment. They rely upon, then, on your mind picking up the subconscious cues, which would then come back to you later, leading to a spike in your curiosity about the product that your favorite celebrity was holding.

Some other product placements are more obvious and in-your-face, yet all rely on your fascination with the people on TV to convince you that using the product would also make you happy, or at least, as cool as your favorite celebrity.

Another way in which advertisers will often manipulate us into buying products or using certain services is through a type of propaganda (more on this later) called bandwagon.

Bandwagon propaganda, as the name suggests, often aims to make people jump into a "bandwagon" as others have. This technique is often used to create emotional cues so as to manipulate people into adopting a certain opinion, or in this case of advertising, into buying a particular product or using a particular service.

This type of manipulation is often used by advertisers to play into our innate desire to be considered part of the crowd. By presenting us with a product and telling us that many people (celebrity endorsements fall into this group) are using the product or service, it creates a desire (emotional cue) in us also to want to become part of the crowd (Bandwagon).

This type of manipulation is also what has led to a spike of the well-known "social media influencers." Visiting several social media sites, you will come across countless of people practicing online influencing.

Because of the value that we, consumers, place in the people that we consider famous or influential, many corporates are finding great success in paying individuals or giving them a product for them to use, in a bid to use the said person's influence to convince the people that put value in that person's opinion buy it.

Then, there is fear. This type of technique is used by advertisers to invoke feelings of dread or a negative consequence if they do not use the product or service that you are selling them. Most often, this technique is used by companies that sell products that reduce risks or improve health.

In an advertisement to sell motorcycle helmets, a helmet company used a testimonial of a supposed survivor of a horrific crash, along with the image of a man with stitching around the side of his head, receiving a tablespoon of medicine from someone off the image. Subtle and poignant. This advert aimed to prey on people's fear of pain and disability to urge them to buy helmets. The advert went further and ran a text at the bottom of the image, revealing the number of fatalities and casualties that were as a result of accidents while not wearing helmets.

Toothpaste companies will often use our fear of bad teeth and bad breath to sell us toothpaste, pointing directly at the food we eat that is left in our teeth as a contributor to the degradation of our teeth. While poor oral hygiene will lead to the degradation of teeth, there are several other contributing factors, such as alcohol consumption, contaminated water, among many others. These, of course, will never be mentioned in the toothpaste commercial, and instead, they will offer the solution to your bad teeth as their toothpaste.

The use of fear is not illegal. However, it is often a requirement that there has to be a risk associated with the product. For example, the risk of poor oral hygiene is bad teeth and bad breath. However, that is not the entire cause.

When advertisers make their adverts, they will often first, go for our basic desires and the fact that there is a barrier to access to these desires. So, for example, a company that wants to sell you pizza will play on the fact that you know if your dietary need is not met, you risk death, and therefore, use that to sell you pizza.

Once that is done, you will get that many advertisers then begin to feed into our trappings for the finer things in life. Through a combination of the bandwagon, bad logic, fear, they then manipulate us into taking their words for it and looking at their product as what we need in our lives to make us happy. They show us images of smiling people supposedly using their product, and that then, feeds into our psyche, leaving us unhappy with what we have and leading us to pursue then the item that they have kept in front of us.

And this all is indeed based on science. Advertisers are no longer just swinging wildly based on their intuition. When psychology as science grew in the early 20th century, along with behavioral sciences later in the century, marketers quickly turned their attention to it.

## Political Manipulation

Looking at people like Adolf Hitler and Joseph Stalin, as well as current US president, Donald Trump, it is hard to understand just how they got to rise to the heights that they are.

The role of media in shaping the political landscape cannot be understated. Thus, whenever you look into both the past and present political climate, many of the people who have taken over power have almost always wanted to control the media. During the heights of dictatorship in many countries, the people in power often sought to muffle the media, through killing or firing of the opposing voices in the media, or would often take control of media as a tool to spread their ideology to the masses, and they would achieve this by creating draconian laws to govern what the media would and wouldn't carry, and by planting people loyal to the people in power control the media rooms.

Indeed, when we look closely, politics has always been a game of manipulation, a way of controlling how people think, and how they act, and thus, how they respond to an authority figure.

Psychologists came up with ways in which governments often affected their manipulation of the people.

Throughout history, many people in power have used bad logic and propaganda to get the people to rally behind them, and indeed, the worst revelations of our psychological horrors came out during this period.

After he seized power, Adolf Hitler created a ministry that was responsible for propaganda. This was so that they could spread their message well to the people of Germany.

So, how did they manage to get to that point? Below, we look at how the governments begin to affect the manipulation techniques.

## Control Attention

Because of the knowledge that people, varied in their experiences and knowledge, would be much harder to control, the Nazi set out to bring the attention of the Germans to specific things that they wanted. By first creating a ministry specifically for propaganda, the Nazis already were lining to turn the eyes of Germans where Adolf Hitler and his fellow commanders wanted them.

Then, once they bring your attention to what they want you to, they repeated the issues. As seen today, Donald Trump continues to reinforce the racist ideologies of the people that voted for him by frequently directing attention towards it, away from other more pressing issues, like the fact that gun crimes have spiked exponentially during his reign.

During their times, Hitler and Stalin often did this through repeated speeches on TVs and podiums, and seeing as they were gifted orators, they were able to easily bring their attention of the people to them and their twisted ideologies.

This modus operandi often uses the element of fear to achieve the desired results. Through fanning people's biases, the leader then makes the population look where they look. The leader's enemies become the people's enemies. Once they achieved, then it is easier to go through the second step.

# Control Perception

Once governments get your attention where they want, they then get around trying to shape how you see things and how you should perceive them.

In the Nazi example, this often involved covering up the atrocities and murders that the government committed and then would manipulate the citizens through the propaganda material, which often included antisemitic material. They would then buy into its racial ideology by making it such that the Jews were inferior beings, and therefore, it was up to them, the German people, to help the government get rid of the Jews. Millions more who could not, or chose not to take part in the atrocities, still managed to be mere bystanders to the targeted murders and persecution. The propaganda had shaped their perception, and thus, made them look at the murders as a responsible counter to the infiltration of the Jews.

In 1944, when the International Red Cross team crossed to Germany to inspect a camp that had been set up for propaganda purposes of the Nazi, the Nazis put up a "beautification program." During their inspection, the SS party produced a propaganda film to show baffled Germans, and the visitors of their benevolence towards the Jewish "residents" of the camp enjoyed. When they finished filming, the people in the camp, who had been put there to give face, were then taken to the Auschwitz-Birkenau killing center.

This tactic also involves repackaging old cues, as well as creating new ones. While racism is now widely frowned upon, many of the emerging extreme political leaders in the world right now are still perpetuating the racial ideologies by waging war against immigrants and other minorities. While not as overt as old times, the targeted verbal attacks are often the leader's means of pulling the attention of their followers.

While we can look at it as something that only bad, racist people do, the same manipulation could still affect all of us, if we got a leader who espoused our deepest beliefs, promised to fulfill our deepest desires, and reinforced our beliefs. This phenomenon is called in psychology "the confirmation bias." Getting a leader who confirms, then reinforces what you already believe as true makes it very easy, then, for them to use that to manipulate you into acting irrationally. Which leads us to the third point

## Reinforcing Old Beliefs

In the Nazi times, the use of films became important in their desire to feed their propaganda to the Germans. Considering that this was a period in time when racial and religious differences were actively leading to large-scale violence, many Germans were probably of the view that Jews, and other races of people, were inferior. To reinforce this, the Nazis then used films such as The Eternal Jew to paint Jews as lesser beings. In the film, the SS party portrayed the Jews as being taken over by money and sex. They were parasites that needed to be kicked out.

This was repeated, and thus, led to further ossifying of the biases view. It also then resorted to swapping the lies with truth and vice versa.

## Create Shared Misery

One of the ways that we see this today is when political leaders begin to act like victims to the people they consider as the "others." Sometime in 2015, South Africa was on the spot for xenophobic attacks against other black foreigners. This then was repeated in 2019, after one of the political leaders claimed that foreigners were taking the jobs of the South African people.

This type of manipulation aims at creating physiological stress on the people that the political leader is manipulating. Once they achieve this, it would then be easier for them to point out at the people that they do not like and say, "there, those people are responsible for your suffering."

Through creating stress to the people that they are wooing, and then pointing out the cause of the misery as an outward force, the political leader can assume the role of savior. When the people do not see an improvement in their living under their savior leader, this creates cognitive stress, further leading them to misery and thus, leading to more of them turning their anger on the people they had been led to believe are responsible for their misery.

Through creating what psychologists call "the mob psychology," the political leader ensures that people do not think too deeply about the real source of their misery, which explains why they remain in power for a long time and seem to hold sway all the while.

## Sell the Outcome

Once Hitler had taken hold of Germans, he was able to maintain his grip by simulating what the world would be like without Jews. He put the Jews away in concentration camps.

This then allowed them to come up with laws that segregated the Jews and other people considered outsiders -the Nuremberg Race Laws. These laws were put in place after Nazi extremists increased violence attacks against the people perceived to be an outsider.

The truth is that many Germans, a good number, in fact, were against the violence against the Jews. However, the propaganda let to the disdain for them spread through many people like a viral infection. This then meant that many Germans passively accepted the discrimination of the Jews and were largely indifference.

Thus, by making violence against Jews and other people the Nazis considered outsiders as something that was necessary and normal to restoring German pride, the SS party was able to get the silent consent of the majority, something that allowed them to thrive then. Such an environment also creates dire consequences for anyone that calls out the political leader for their harmful philosophy. Thus, though unwittingly, most people in such a case end up in the bandwagon, going on with the flow of the others in the fear that the party and their supporters would victimize them.

When a political leader creates an environment where their word is law, and there are consequences to the contrary, it then begins a terrible cycle where their most radical followers then begin to act like mobs against those that disagree with the leader. Such vicious mob psychology has often lead to the worst acts committed by people against other people.

This is what allowed Belgian King and war criminal King Leopold to kill millions in Congo. It is what allowed Idi Amin Dada to kill hundreds in Uganda with barely a conscience.

As we see above, the darkness in the human psychology comes out better when politics and advertisement, the two major places where we want to feel as "part of the crowd."

While we look at the dark tendencies of serial killers as things unique to them, the historical revelation that many people would commit depraved acts if they felt that there would be no consequences for their actions prove that indeed, while we have our inhibitions, we aren't incorruptible, and that the only mistake serial killers do is make it a habit.

# Chapter 7: Advanced Manipulation Techniques that Only 3% of the World Population Know

Various manipulation techniques are used by sociopaths and narcissists as well as psychopaths to exert an individual control over their victims. It is worth noting that as human beings, there are chances that one has ever utilized manipulation at some point. In other words, people use white lies to get out of a situation or somewhat flatter so as one may get what they want. Thus, manipulation is one of the tools that is used by different people as their first tool in an arsenal of techniques critical in overpowering their victims. In other words, narcissists, as well as people in power, uses manipulation techniques to win the confidence of their victims and emerge victors in their persuasion. The predators also use these manipulative techniques to control their victims, and in most cases, they target a specific type of individual. Thus, if you are a person of low self –esteem, there are chances that these people will easily manipulate you and utilize your efforts to make their goals.

Take a look at some of the manipulation techniques that only 3% of the world population know:

## Lying

The art of lying has been one of the manipulative methods used by predators in every aspect of their lives.

Predators lie such that their victims trust them and get confused. Lying has been the significant manipulation technique that psychopaths use to typically introducing some imaginations to victims. Most of these predators will promise heaven while they understand that none- of such promises are practical.

In most cases, they will identify the weakness of their victims and work on them. They will lie about issues that don't exist and promise to fulfill or supply items that will never be available. One of the aspects that is critical about these predators is that they will use all schemes to approach their victims and use the first few minutes to learn and try to identify the aspects that are affecting their victims. They will then use money or anything else that will serve their victims for their favor. For instance, they will buy lunch or anything that will keep their victims confused. At times, some will lie on their achievements as a means of winning the confidence of their victims. They will pump their victims with issues that are 100% lies, yet they pretend as if they own or have utilized time to win whatever they have. The aspect confuses through victims who later use more than what they have as they try to gain the confidence of their persuaders. In other words, the victims get confused such that they will submit anything they own as they can achieve the empty promises offered.

## Not Telling the Entire Story

The art of leaving a victim in suspense is critical in the sense that it leaves them at one's advantage. In other words, manipulators, as well as predators, don't say everything. The victims aren't allowed to understand what is happening at large. The aspect is linked to the fact that if the entire Story is narrated, there are chances that the truth might be identified, and the predators might suffer. One of the aspects that causes predators to hide some accounts is the fact that they target lying to win. In other words, there is no way they can lie to their victims and tell everything. The aspect is critical in the sense that the more they speak, the more they can easily confuse themselves and end up losing following the revelation of truth. The art of being in suspense causes their victims to follow them hence more manipulated.

## Frequent Mood Swings

The aspect of understanding one's attitude is essential. That is understanding when happy and when one is angry. However, it is tough to understand the moods of these manipulators. They pretend to be always satisfied as a means of winning the confidence of their victims. The art of pretending to be happy is critical in confusing their victims with empty promises. For instance, they may pretend to be satisfied, yet they might be suffering. The aspect is crucial in the sense that is causing their victims to think that everything that the manipulators say is turn, and they end up losing their properties to them.

## Love-bombing and Devaluation

Narcissists are typically love bombing, and they will charm some offensive techniques in the name of love. In other words, they will hook up with their victims and offer them more love and protection. The victims get carried away and drop all the items they are asked as a means of protecting this love. The predators will use their funds to ensure that they have blinded their victims with much love. They, in most cases, identify places where they won't easily be identified. At times, they recognize the hotels or restaurants that are expensive so as they can take their victims as a way of hiding their truth in them. Some may offer to help their victims achieve more and earn more in the name of love. However, they will do this as they hide their identity and as they increase their approach towards winning and getting their primary target.

## Punishment

Manipulators use sought of punishment as a means of proving their point. They will keep nagging until they get what they want. In other cases, they may shout or use the silent treatment or instead physically punish their victims for achieving what they need. The aspect is critical in the sense that it hides their identity as they appear to be more exact. Mental abuse has been one of the significant damage that has been used by a lot of manipulators to confuse their victims. In most cases, the victims will feel tortured and feel like there is nothing left rather than submitting to these manipulators for the sake of their peace.

## Denial

Denial is the common means that manipulators use when they are caught lying. They will never accept that they have committed a particular claim. When caught up in chaos, or when their plans backfire, they are quick to deny and probably transfer the blame to the victim. They reject all the aspects they are accused of and assumes that nothing has been happening.

## Spinning the Truth

Have you ever listened and watched how politicians twist facts and truths to suit them, this is precisely what manipulators do. In other words, they will combine all the facts about and twist lies and end up winning. In other words, if they are discovered to have lied in one way or another, they are quick in twisting the truth and speaking only the things that favor them. It is one of the worst behaviors of these predators. The aspect is linked to the fact that in one way or another, these truths are identified, and they may end up losing in the long run.

## Minimizing

In most cases, the manipulators will try and play down their actions as a way of shifting the damage and end-up, moving the blame to the victims for over-reacting. In other words, when things backfire, that is quick in under-estimating the cost, or somewhat the losses incurred. In other cases, they shift the blame to the victims, especially when they have made a few mistakes in the process. There are cases where they pretend to be compensating for the loses in the name of, love as they work for their primary target. They will thus minimize the efforts of the victims and call for more shots and end up winning in the long run. However, if their plans are identified, they are quick to deny and minimize the ideas of the victims as well. The approach is critical in the sense that it offers the best means of escaping or hiding from the truth.

## Plays the Victim

One of the aspects that have been utilized by a good number of manipulators is the art of playing as victims. In other words, if there is a situation that involved their plans, they will act like victims, so others may have compassion and sympathy. It is worth noting that as human beings, the art of giving and helping those or rather the suffering is an art. In other words, human beings will always give to the poor as well as these in enormous pain. Thus manipulators take advantage of the situation, play as the most victimized by circumstances, and end up gaining or achieving their target.

## Targeting their Victims

All the activities or the plans that manipulators have is that of targeting the victim. In most cases, they accuse the victims of wrongdoing. In the long run, the victim defends themselves as they expose their properties as well as secrets. The focus is, in most cases, on the victims rather than the accuser. Thus, the manipulator will ensure that the victim has exposed all their secrets. They will then use some of these secrets as well as a weakness as a means of achieving all that they want. For instance, the victim may be forced to reveal some of the secrets about their source of funds as well as security passwords that safeguard these funds. The predators may then secretively take or use what they have been aiming at long last.

## Positive Enforcement

Most predators are experts in this area. For instance, they will buy expensive presents, praise the victims or instead give money to the victims as they try to win the confidence of their victims. In other words, they have behaviors that are aimed at pleasing their victims and confusing them as well. In most cases, they keep apologizing and have excessive charms as they pay lots of attention to the victims. The aspect is critical in the sense that it confuses the victims such that they are left wondering where else they can receive such treatment. However, when they are complicated to the latter, the manipulators will use their deceptive schemes to acquire what they were aiming at and leave the victims in suffering. In most cases, that will escape avoiding being questioned by the victims on recovery.

## Moving the Goal Posts

Most of the predators will keep shifting their target from one point to the other. In other words, the predators will set goals and attempt to offer some help to the victims. However, on the verge of achieving these goals, the predator will change them and shift the focus. The aspect confuses the victim, and they will keep chasing the target and getting more confused. The element is critical in the sense that it keeps the victim pursuing empty promises and goals that will never be achieved. However, as the victims run after their gals, the predators utilize this opportunity.

## Diversion

The art of diverting ideas has been utilized by manipulators to confuse their victims. In other words, different people will keep shifting from one aspect of communication to the other so as the minds of the victim might be opened and identify some of the false found in these predators. In other words, predators will not allow the victim to concentrate on specific issues, as this might be the only secret they have. Thus, they will try and make their victims busy and prevent them from taking a particular line of thought. The art is critical in the sense that it emotions the victim, and they are left confided and wonder which path to take. When the victims are confused, the predators utilize this moment to lead their victims into areas where they are easily swayed and denied their rights as well. Their properties might be robbed as the predators get what they have been looking for.

## Sarcasm

One of the aspects that makes predators appear to be more superiors. The element is linked to the fact that the predators prefer when they are in command. Thus, the predators will ensure that if you have low –self-esteem, you will need them more. Therefore, they might abuse you or be sarcastic in front of others. The aspect allows them to show how powerful they are and how disadvantaged the victims are. In the long run, the victims have to depend on the predators for survival. The aspect remains to be the primary target of predators where the victim will keep seeking guidance from them. In the long run, they will the victims to ensure that they have benefitted at the end of the day.

## Flattery

As human beings, if one is praised, you feel useful and vital. Most of the predators have identified this aspect had have been utilizing it to win the confidence of most of these victims. In most cases, the predator will keep praising their victims, telling them how good they are as a means of winning their trust. In other cases, the victim is naturally made to be happy and receive relatively false compliments and those that are aimed at achieving specific goals. The victim is prepared to accept that whatever they are thinking or doing is okay and that they are in the best option. However, before they realize that they have been flattered, predators have already found their way out of their lives, having stolen what they needed.

# Playing Innocent Cards

A real manipulator is always shocking and can't have easily been identified. In other words, they know how to hide their identity and are, in most cases, realized to be predators after they have acquired what they wanted and paved their way out. The aspect is linked to the fact that they will pretend to be innocents and act as the primary victims. Some will assume regular jobs or start working in a certain way as a means of winning the confidence of their victims. They have sweet words that tend to confuse their victims, as well. They also behave well such that their behaviors or even tricks will never be applied. They, in most cases, pretend to have nothing going on well, yet they are the best planners. They may even kill a –resins and remain in the same environment, and no one will accuse or suspect them following their innocence of doing things. They utilize their ability to lie and find confusing stories. The aspect allows predators to escape and find means of surviving even in places they aren't known.

# Isolation

It is worth noting that if a person is confined in a particular environment, there are chances that they will be easily be manipulated as compared to when they gave their family members who might offer some hints here and there. However, predators understand that if victims are isolated in a particular environment, they will readily be confided, and it will be easier to manipulate them. However, on realizing or identifying the major weakness of the victim, the manipulator takes advantage of being caring and lovely to the victim. In the long run, the victim may end up suffering as they may realize they are conned while the accuser has already been identified.

## Feigns of Love and Empathy

One of the aspects that is worth noting is that predators, psychopaths don't know how to love someone or rather respect others. It is hard to feel empathy for them. In most cases, they prefer a situation where they are the ones to be given all the credit. However, if they are manipulative, they will allow to be compassionate and have empathy so as they can win the confidence of their victims. Such manipulative techniques will enable them to gain access to their victims and achieve what they want.

The art of being manipulative is delicate. It requires one to be vigilant and careful not to display their true identity before their mission is complete. In other words, if one is acting as a predator will hide their status until they have acquired what they wanted. In most cases, the victims are left with the role of identifying that they were coned after the manipulators have left. The manipulators may join an individual and start working with them. They may even spend a lot of time to study and identify their victims so as they can easily manipulate them. It is worth noting that since they chose victims that behave with relatively low-self-esteem, they will start by offering presents as well as positive adjustments that will help them rise and feel appreciated. The predators may also provide presents as well as monetary funds as a means of winning the confidence of their victims. In the long run, one they have invested in creating a good rapport between them and their victims. The aspect is critical in the sense that it allows the victim to trust the manipulators and share some of the confidant information. In the long run, the victims are easily manipulated as they have already trusted such an individual.

It is worth noting that these manipulators will lie all over and deny having committed any mistake. In the long run, the manipulators promise heaven in an unrealistic world. It is worth noting that after the identity of the predators is known, the victims are already in regrets. The aspect is linked to the fact that after denial, and revelation, the predator may leave the victim in tears. The trust gained lowers immediately, and one feels betrayed. It is worth noting that most of these predators prefer the art of creating friendship and trust at first.

In most cases, the victims easily trust the manipulators who take san advantage without their knowledge. The truth is, in most cases, identified after the predators' leaves secretary. The art is linked to the fact that most if these manipulators have an aim that keeps driving them. In other words, their manipulation tends to be directed towards having a specific goal. Thus, the significant role of these manipulators is to ensure that they have identified a target, worked in it and caved it by manipulating others. Manipulation has been the making strategy used in winning confidence if more clients.

# Chapter 8: The Subtle Art of Deception

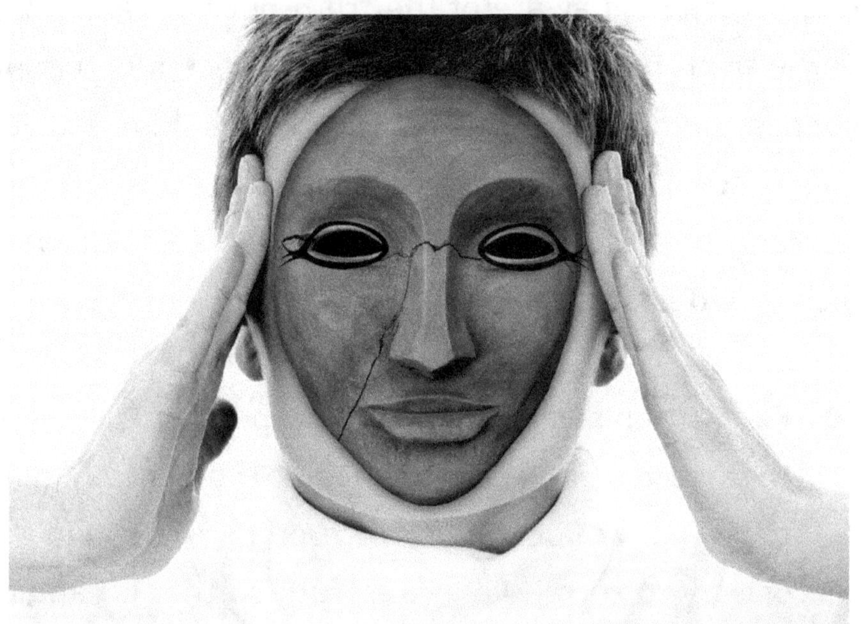

There are ways people use deception; sometimes, the deception is self-deception, while at other times, other people deceive someone else for selfish gains like money or getting confidential information that should not be shared.

Self-deception does not only involve lying to ourselves but also consists of the mind playing tricks on us. With lying, someone is aware of the truth but chooses not to use the truth but instead lie while self-deception people convince themselves unconsciously that a lie is a truth. In self-deception, a person does not realize when they are telling a lie. There are various types of self-deception which include:

1. Functional self-deception – a person will lie to themselves and even go ahead to convince himself that what he just did is not wrong. A person in this will try to turn a lie into a truth so that it can suit them best. A person who continues to continually deceive themselves this way does not face any risks because they will not see the need for taking a chance no matter how beneficial the risk is. They will convince themselves that the risk is not worth taking.

2. Value and believe - a person here deceives themselves that the more expensive something is, the more valuable it is. They place worthiness at the value level. If something does not seem valuable to them, they will not go for it. This might make such a person continue chasing things that are valuable but not helpful to them. They think the difficult it is to attain it the worthy it is, so much time may be lost while trying to get something that wasn't going to help them in any way.

3. Consolatory self-deception - in this, somebody refuses to be accountable for anything and instead continually tries to find the nearest person to blame for everything. For such people, nothing is ever their fault; it's always the other person's fault that something didn't work in a certain way. Such a person is unlikely ever to face their problems because they do not acknowledge them, to begin with.

4. Lying to others to assure yourself is also another form of self-deception. You tend to make small lies when talking to people until the lies become your truth somehow. Such people lie to others until they also end up forgetting what the truth was, to

begin with. The lie becomes so real that even the truth now becomes a lie. The mind somehow captures the dishonesty, and therefore, the truth is easily forgotten.

The other deception, which is very dangerous involves offenders trying to deceive people in a criminal way. The scammers will get their targeted victims, who will cheat and up sometimes robbing them of a lot of money, getting very confidential information, and sometimes even risking the victim's life. Such offenders are criminals who are continually sought after by the law enforcers. Sometimes they are able to get away with it but at the expense of living the victim in a tragedy of loss and having to deal with the recovery of whatever they have lost from the perpetrators.

Art of deception has been well mastered by some individuals to exploit people into disclosing confidential and personal information, which may be used for scheming purposes. The art of deception is a way of brainwash people to achieve a sure selfish thing. It involves social engineering manipulation, which is the psychological tricking of other people for them to do or disclose their personal information. A lot of malicious activities happen when people interact. People are tricked into making security errors and giving out the very sensitive information that may work against them in the long run.

Social engineering attacks happen when people take a lot of sensitive issues for granted. An offender will first carry out his investigation on his targeted victim and gather as much information as he could get. The information may include social security details that the victim doesn't think is very important. The offender will then try to befriend the victim and gain his trust before proceeding to expose the information by either releasing it or sharing with other sources that may have hired him.

## The Attacks May Involve the Following Life Cycle

- Preparation – an offender gets their intended victim, gets all the information needed to base the attack, finds the best strategy or method to carry out the attack.
- Approach – making friends with the intended victim, faking a believable story so that the victim may be free with them,

- Gathering more information – this involves tricking the already made friend who is the victim to give more additional information, delivery of the attack after all the information has been collected, and there is no loophole, destruction of data.

- Sealing the deal - the offender erases any evidence that may tie him to the crime, covers all the track to ensure that his attack is not easily traceable, Making a natural exit as if nothing happened and as if he is not aware of anything related to those activities.

- The most dangerous aspect of this whole social engineering thing is that it is dependent on human mistakes or recklessness. The software and operating system are highly efficient, but when somebody makes a mistake, there is nothing that can prevent this attack from happening. It is very difficult to predict human errors and, therefore, the vulnerabilities.

- Social engineering can happen at any time, anywhere in the world, as long as there is human interaction. Below is a list of some of the most and widely known social engineering attacks that exist.

# Social Engineering Techniques

- Baiting is a deliberate attempt to try and provoke someone or something. Baiting attacks involve giving fake promises to provoke the greed or curiosity of the victim. A victim is lured into a trap where their information is stolen, or their system is inflicted with malware. The most common type of baiting involves the use of media to distribute malware. An example of this is when an offender intentionally put a malware-infected flash where the victim is most likely to access like in a mall, in the washrooms, or parks where the victim can quickly get hold of it. The bait has an original look and has a label that may indicate things that the victim is most likely to be interested in. When the victim picks up the flash, and due to curiosity inserts the flash inside a home or work computer, there will be an automatic installation of the malware on the system.

- Scareware involves constant scaring of people with false alarms or fabricated threats. The victim is made to think that his system has a malware infection, which may make them install software that is not really needed for the victim but may be useful to the offender or even be deceived into installing the malware itself without them realizing that it is malware. Scareware is also called deception software or "Fraudware." The most famous or used shareware includes the pop-up banners that pop up on someone's browser when they are on the screen that screams that the computer is infected and may need to be cleaned. What the pop-up banner offers a person is the installation of a tool that may be malware of may be infected with malware. You may also be directed to a site that has infections, and when you get to the site, the computer now becomes infected. Often scareware is distributed as a pop-up banner in the mails as a spam mail or even as a buy offer to buy things online with very low prices or even in the form of very catchy promotions. If someone does all or one of the above, their computer will be infected.

- Pretexting – the deception here is wisely crafted with trickery lies involved. An offender will trick the victim by engaging them and asking for sensitive, confidential information so that the offender can be able to perform a specific task for the victim. Usually, the task includes something that may help the victim. To be able to achieve this, the attacker will first try to engage the victim by impersonation. They may pretend to be a family member, friend, co-worker, police, bank official, or any person with authority to make such inquisitions. The offender will begin by asking questions that are intended to gather a victim's real identity from which they will then be able to gather confidential information. The pretext may ask questions about the social number details pretending to be the police, and later use the features to access all the data belonging to the victim. This scam is used to gather the most detailed information that is supposed to be a top-secret, and that could quickly bring a person down. The information may include social number details, bank statements, personal address, personal number, phone's recording, and even information that gives a person their security. With this information lying on the wrong hands, destruction is very easy, and that's why it is essential to be sure of who you are sharing your details with.

- Phishing is one of the most well-known social engineering attack types. Phishing involves mail, text messages that are intended to create a sense of fear, curiosity, and urgency to the victims. When the victims are at this phase of fear and curiosity, the offender makes the victim reveal their most sensitive information by clicking on links of the most dangerous websites or even by accessing malware-infected websites. The example of this scam is an online service provider tricks the user into thinking that they have violated the policy and need an essential password change with immediate effect. To change the password, one is required to follow a specific link that usually leads them to a dangerous website that looks exactly as the real website or the actual legit version of the site, and then the victim will be trusting enough to enter the relevant information plus password. Once this information is fed on the website its sent and immediately gets to the offender, since most of these scam emails are usually the same or most likely to be the same, and only changed in several areas to make them seem more authentic and yet sent to everyone, it's very easy for them to be detected and blocked before they get to a lot of innocent victims. The mail servers should try tracing them so that they are blocked on time because they have access to threat sharing forums.

- Spear phishing is a version of the phishing scam, and attackers in this scam choose specific individuals or companies. They fake the messages based on a person's well-known identity or character, positions they hold at their workplace, and people that the victim well knows so that it is easily believable. Spearfishing requires so much time and work for the attacker and takes longer for the attacker to implement. This is because it is harder for them to gather everything and also apply, although it's also the best rewarding method for the attacker. A spear-phishing attack may involve someone pretends to be the company's IT guy, and he may send emails to a specific or several employees. The mail is written precisely as an IT guy would and also have the same signature as the IT guy. It is, therefore, very easy for the mail recipients to think it's an authentic message because of how detailed and genuine it looks. The email may persuade the recipients to change their password by following a link that the offender intends them to follow for them to be able to capture the company's details. There are several ways that people can avoid and stop this kind of scams.

- Vishing – sometimes, the attackers are not always using the internet to scam, but then other scammers will use the phone calls. What the scammers will do is create an interactive voice response system of a certain company. They will then manipulate people to call using the toll-free number. When people fall into this trick, they will enter their details before making the calls, and therefore, the attackers will get access to their information in this way.

- Tailgating – Here, attackers will get help from someone on the inside who can access the information on their behalf or even who can tip them on various issues.

- Quid pro quo – this involves people impersonating the technical support team. They will make calls to a particular company and pretend to be trying to solve a technical issue. The offender will try to solve un existing hitches through the phone call by making the victim do precisely as they want or intend them to. This kind of scam involves a reward from the offender in exchange for the information they will get.

## Social Engineering Prevention

Social engineering is a scam intended to manipulate people by playing with their emotions by creating fear or curiosity for the attackers to be able to gather information. There are, therefore, cautions that a person can take in order to avoid these scams. Emails received should be taken with great caution, reading, analyzing, and getting to know every detail before acting on them. Be alert of all the pop-ups, promotions or adverts, and any digital information that is just at the disposal.

**Improving emotional intelligence** is the most significant prevention of any manipulation. The attackers will try to play with your emotions; what they most want from you is to make you fearful, guilty, and anxious. A person with high emotional intelligence cannot be played in this manner and is therefore safe from manipulation.

**Be cautious of your environment** before accessing your account or any activity on the internet. One glance at your computer from the wrong person might significantly expose your confidential information.

**Avoid and stop opening emails from sources that are not well known to you**. If you are not familiar with the sender, you should not feel obligated to reply to an mail. And even though you know the sender but the message seems suspicious, or you do not understand the message, it's good to do a follow up before acting on the mail. To do this confirmation, you may call them through their phones to hear directly from them, or instead of following the link; you should go directly to the server's original site to be sure. It's good to always remember that emails are hacked all the time, and even though the source of the email may be genuine, he may have been hacked himself, and the attackers used his mail to scam you.

**Multifactor method** – the essential information for an attacker is user credentials. The multifactor authentication enables a person to secure their account so that in case the system is compromised; your mind is still safe. The security information of the report should always be safeguarded.

**Being careful of all those too good to be genuine offers is very important**. Attackers know how to play with your mind, and suggestions are very enticing. Next time before you click an offer link, it's good to pause and think because you might be protecting yourself from a massive scam. You may decide to look the offer up on google to find out if the offer is indeed genuine or not.

**Keeping your computer's antivirus updated is also very important.** Regularly updating the antivirus should be a norm or downloading a new antivirus on a daily basis. Then the next thing should be continually checking the computers to make sure that the system has no infections.

Attackers are very daring because they will get a person's phone number and make the victim the most irresistible offer. They are very friendly because they intend to make you trust them. Sometimes they will ask the victims for money in order for the victim to get the offer, which is usually much valuable than the money they are asking for. This art of deception is called a Fraud. But then the extreme of deception is when attackers decide to use psychological games of deceit with the victim who is now the social engineering.

Sometimes attackers do not just manipulate for financial gains. Sometimes the attackers will manipulate to gather information. This manipulation sometimes involves even having your friends manipulating you for them to access your password.

# Chapter 9: Become a Real Mind Hacker

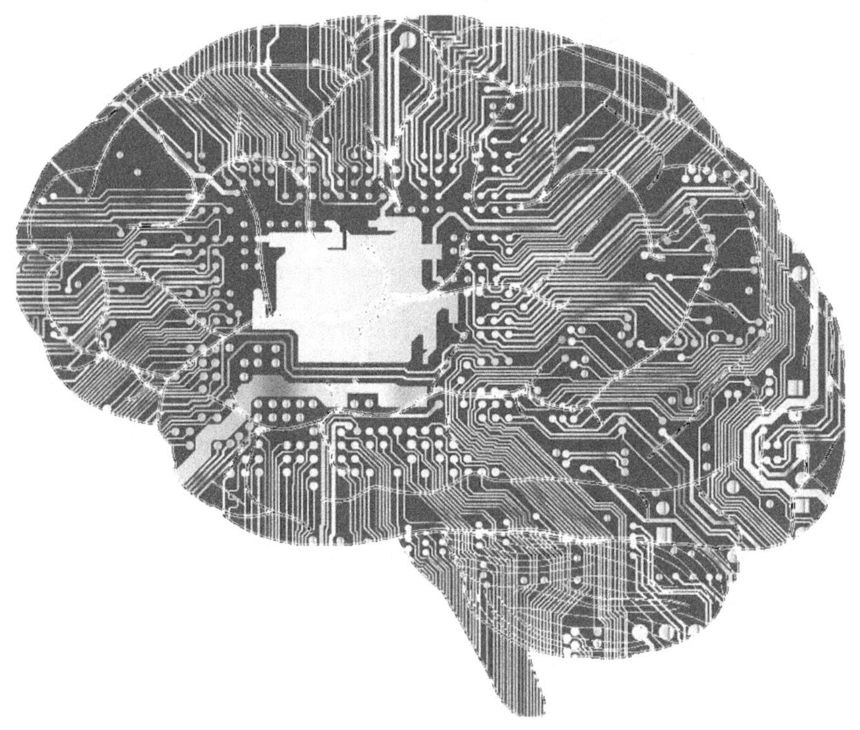

Most of you already know who a hacker is. We mostly know them from the world of computers. We already know that hackers are people who try to get into a system that is not theirs. In computer hacking, it is trying to get into a system to get information or even cash if the system has cash in it. They get in through codes they formulate, which may be called encryptions to the system. These encryptions just have to bypass the firewall of the passcode of the system that they are trying to get into. So the mind hacker is no different from the computer hacker. The only difference is that the computer hacker deals with computers while the mind hacker deals with the mind. The mind is just like a computer; it is the central command of the whole body. Hacking into the brain need encryptions, just like in computer hacking. The encryptions are the tactics to get to your brain. The tactics than have to pass a firewall, which is the chain system of the brain's passcode. With this knowledge, then hacking into the brain is not as hard as it sounds.

So what are the ways you can make your mind open? There are so many ways to open the mind. Once you open your mind, then it is easy to hack into it or for someone else to do that. The first would be meditation. Meditation is the process of clearing the mind, body, and soul. That means that one becomes free of their thoughts, feelings, and emotions too. It lets someone open up as a way of being free. It involves the body, soul, and mind, which work together harmoniously. To reach one, then you must also reach the other. When the mind is free, you can be able to deal with anything. Your thoughts become clear, and your life just opens itself. There is the option of opening your life to new ideas and perspectives too. Meditation helps you be calm and to be able to plan the next step without any hindrance due to the clarity you already have. To have a peaceful and calm life, try and meditate once in a while, it helps. You can reach your inner thoughts and feelings if you would like to just by meditation.

Another way of reaching through your mind is through music. So people ask themselves how does music help, and all I can say is that you should know that it does. Music has been recently found to be a good source of therapy. Every genre of music has an effect on someone. Like happy songs make you cheery, and you feel like dancing and singing. Sad songs make you reflect on your own life; some even try to compare themselves to the songs. Rock music makes you feel like you are on top of the world. As for house or electric, you feel free like the music has taken over you or something like that. Slow songs with a calming effect are just to keep you relaxed. Most of the hypnosis psychiatrists are believed to use music in their therapy sessions. Music is like a healer and a guide. When you are lost or do not know the way, then music is there to help. Music is beloved by almost everyone, thus an easy tactic to use. It can be made from anything and everything. It consists of chords that make it up. These chords from A to G, these are the most popular ones.

Also, there is walking and listening to nature. People have forgotten all about nature; they have even forgotten how beautiful it is. Nature opens up your mind and helps to keep you calm. The scenery that nature brings out is so nice that all you do is getting drawn to it. This means that one is captivated, and the only thoughts you have are of what you see. As you take in everything, then your mind continues to open. This is the time you can notice the little things you never noticed before. All the things that were not clear at a certain point become very clear, and you become very calm and less confused. This is a very easy task that is not expensive at all. All you have to do is get out a little. I am sure most of the small or minor things around where you live you will notice them for the very first time. It does not have to be a long walk or a tour to somewhere far. The only thing to note is that it has to be a new adventure for you to take on. Be free, be wild, and open your mind.

The final one, of course, is the known one, which is therapy. Therapy is in so many forms, but the ones that affect the mind are cognitive, psychoanalysis, and psychoanalytic too. All these types of therapy work differently. Although psychoanalysis and psychoanalytic are similar, both have some differences in their beliefs. The founder of psychoanalytic, who was Erik Erickson, just added to the work of psychoanalysis' founder Sigmund Freud. Cognitive therapy looks at the mind works, and with these hacking into the mind is easy. As for psychoanalysis and psychoanalytic, both look at the unconscious mind. For both therapies, there can be the use of hypnosis. This can be used to uncover thoughts, secrets, and even past forgotten events. With these, you can be able to understand your mind or others' minds and how they work. To get to someone's brain then that is the firewall you must cross for the hacking to work. Therapy is to help you get through your problems and at the very end, they should your guide to a better life. These should be less hustle and with more clarity of what you want as the mind has new programming.

## Ways to Hack the Brain

The first is to smell nice. This helps to boost your self-confidence. When you are meeting up with other people, one usually puts on deodorant or even spray themselves. The question is, why do we do that? This is easy; it is all in the mind. If we believe that we smell nice, we feel like we are at the top. That means we feel nice about ourselves. It ensures that we feel very confident in the activities we are going to undertake. Once we show confidence, then others see us in the same light. All that matters is how you see yourself. Then the others will see you in the same light without hesitation. You are the starter. You are the leader of your own life, and the rest have to follow you. So smelling nice is just but one the ways to boost your self-confidence. Every time you go out to smell nice, take charge, and believe that you smell nice. With this, you can make someone think how confident you are. This trick can be used on friends, family, and even in a dating scenario. If you want to hide the shyness from others, this then is a great trick. It helps you see things like you are in a high position. It grants you the power of self-confidence in all that you are planning to do with other people that are around you. Also smelling nice is just a good trait to have.

The other thing is to know how to reduce the pain. When we are hit by something, we are bound to feel the pain. Studies have shown we only feel pain when we look at the wound or cut or the bruised area. This means that we can avoid pain if we want to. It is all in one's mind on the pain issue. This is when the binoculars come in. It helps one to avoid having as much pain as he or she usually has. That means that one is forced to look at the wound they have but in a smaller size. As the wound reduces in size, so does the pain. The pain also increases as soon as you see the wound as a big thing. This is one way to look at it and to deal with the physical pain, but there is also another way. In this way, the facts are not looking at the wound or bruise or even cut. People think you cannot assume the pain, but you actually can. Pain is perceived on the body, and pain receptors send the message to the brain. What if stopping this whole process is possible? The only thing we need to cut off is the perceived pain. This is where the assuming part comes in. As you assume the wound or bruise, there is no message that is sent to the brain, and then there is no pain that ends up being felt in the long run.

Also, there is the fact of having a wild imagination. This is when you can dream of something you really wanted in the end. That means seeing not in a dream state as you are asleep, this is picturing all that you want. Everyone wants good things in life; then, everyone's imagination is bound to be very good. It helps you to push your dreams into a reality. Most kids and young people are told to have an active imagination. This is to help out in building the futures that are ahead of them. In your imagination, you can see anything you wish to. You can take control of the story since it is your own make ensure that the imagination is per what you wanted — an imagination running wild means that you are very creative. You can then get out of any mess that you are in. After having this wild imagination, the next step is to make it come alive. This is through hard work and ensuring that you achieve all the goals you are setting. The imaginations you have do not let them be just imaginations. Imaginations exist to push you forward. They make you realize that all the dreams you have can happen if you just push yourself a little forward. Do not just be a dreamer expand your mind, and also who you are. Well, success is all from the mind, and imaginations are just but a trigger to those successes.

Another way is by ensuring that your memory is good. In most people, it is hard to remember things. In the past few years, it was only a problem associated with the old, but nowadays the young are affected too. This is because we have all become too busy. The number of responsibilities has increased in all levels of life, whether you are young or old, it does not matter. So how do we increase our memories? Current people have made lists and programs to remind them, but the truth of the matter is that these are not mind-based, and they only help us in knowing what to follow and not to increase our memories. What if the list was erased and could not be traced back then most of us would not remember the things they ought to do at the time. This then brings me to the idea that I have that could help the situation. So in the ancient city of Greece and Rome came up with a perfect way to improve human memory. This way was what they called the mind palace. What is the mind palace? The mind palace is a big map that one should design in their heads. It should have all the places that affect your life. It helps one to set like a timetable for each day with each activity that they are doing. This keeps track of everything, and since it is set in the mind, it is pretty much hard to forget the routine.

The other way is by knowing how to use your eyebrows. Some people just think that the eyebrows are just there. Others also think that eyebrows are just there to sweep off the dust to prevent it from reaching the eye area.

The eyebrow does not only have that to do. It can be used in communication. This is what is called body language, or in this case, the facial language. It is a non-verbal type of conversation. One can communicate with others without necessarily using words to do it, and it works as good word of mouth. With the eyebrows, you can raise them during the conversation. This is especially appropriate when you disagree with their point. It is better than interrupting someone as they talk. Raising your eyebrows helps you to disagree but in a silent mode. This is perceived as less rude, unlike interrupting, when one is talking. In this case, one waits their turn to disagree. There is also another way to communicate in this category, which is widening or squinting of the eyes. Widening of the eyes is mostly associated with disbelief and shock. This is where you do not believe in what someone is saying, and this is a gesture to show what you feel. There is also the squinting; it also is associated with disbelief but not a shock as the widening of the eyes has been seen. Shock is the state of being stunted by someone's actions or, better yet their words.

Also, there are writing things so that you can easily remember. This is mostly used by students. They are advised to jot down something as they read if they want to fully understand what they have read. That means that this is some good advice. We do not have photographic memories; this is why we have to write down the important facts. This is to ensure that you can easily remember. Studies have shown that students who jot down something as they read are better performing, unlike those who do not write anything as they read. When you get to the exam room, and a question that you studied for pops up you were writing something as you were reading, you will remember what you wrote down thus you will be able to answer the question that has been given to you in the test. Although it is a good thing and opens up the memory for some people, it just does not click in. For some, just reading is enough for them. Writing this should be a habit everyone learns since we cannot remember everything that is put ahead of us. Tests may make us nervous and make us forget all we have put in our minds. All we can really on is the pictures of the memories as we write these important points. There is more to it like the writing, what should I write, and what should I not? The important thing is writing the things that you may forget.

The second last point is that one should avoid choking. I know you are wondering why I am talking about choking. Chocking is not only about food or water; it is much more than that. In this case, I may call it freezing up and not choking. Now I know you get the point now. Freezing up is something that happens to us, especially if we are in front of a big crowd. Freezing up, just like in all the points that I have discussed is all in the mind. It is, therefore, something we can control. It is majorly caused by us second-guessing ourselves instead of us just doing what we want to do. We keep asking ourselves how others will see us. This is where we go wrong because our opinions are what should come first before the others have any other say. This leads us to have low self-esteem, and so we cannot face others. We also forget the reason we were going to perform in front of others, which hinders us from being ourselves at that point and time. This is something I have experienced myself, and to be honest, it was all in my head. I was so afraid of singing in front of others even though I knew I had a magnificent voice. At that time, it did not matter. Once I put the thoughts aside and sang, then the fear was all gone, and I could be me again.

Finally is to avoid stress. This is where one is challenged by life so hard that they have a lot of things in their minds. So what are we supposed to do when our thoughts are the only things that are around us? The first thing is to take a break. I know people hear of this every day. It is all in the mind; all the thoughts are stored and run from there. So taking a break is telling your mind to stop. Once you tell your mind to stop, take up activities that make you very happy, and that keep you smiling through and through. Laughing is seen to be another cure for stress. It seems far-fetched but it is a good cure for stress and all those negative things that are in your life already. So how does laughter help in reducing stress? As one laughs, you feel like there are surges of electricity in your body — not the bad kind of electricity but the good kind. The more you look at it, something funny that makes you smile always brightens your day no matter how bad the day might have been. The person who said laughter is like medicine was not wrong at all. You have to laugh to feel better since life is not very easy. It is a very rocky and bumpy road. So these are ways in which you can hack into your brains and others' too if you like. These are very practical ways that are very simple to follow.

# Conclusion

Thank you for reaching the end of the book. So far, through the whole book, we have looked at dark psychology. That means looking into what dark psychology is and all of its aspects. We have seen that dark psychology already has a very long past tried to do it. We have seen that it has evolved as the years passed that are for the purpose of it going with the times. Change is inevitable, and dark psychology is no different. The book totally gave more information than what I am trying to summarize here.

So, in conclusion, the book focused on many things. One of these things was the dark triad, which consists of three aspects. The one that is mostly known of the three is narcissism. Narcissism happens to us all the time from different people. Narcissistic people are very self-centered. The only thing they care about is themselves and well their prosperity too. They have to find a way to get to the top, and they have to do that through other people. The simply push people around to get their goals. They care less about who they hurt in the long run.

Another thing that was discussed was the political and historical ways people used dark psychology. It looks keenly on the ways historical politicians used dark psychology in governing their subjects. The question have you ever wondered how they got away with everything was finally answered in this chapter. This chapter opens our eyes to politics and how each and every time we are deceived by our own leader. In most countries, these leaders are whom we have voted in. That seems very cliché, but the truth of the matter is that we become pawns in their own little and silly games.

There were also advanced techniques to manipulate others. As said before there is only 3% of people who have mastered the art of manipulation. Why manipulation is known as art is due to the fact that it is something that is acquired over time. Manipulation enables one to get what they want in the end. This is making someone believe in the course you want them to take. It is mostly confused with persuasion, which is totally different. Persuasion is where you use works to convince someone to do something for you, and at the very end, you make sure that they do it.

Finally, there was also the talk of mind hacking in which someone is able to tap into their mind or others' minds. It helps one figure and solves their problems. In the case where it is used on others, one is able to take control and make things go their way. There is so much more to mind hacking like ways to do so and how to become good at mind hacking. This is just but the summary of what you have already looked at in the book. This is what the book had to offer, but there is more to dark psychology since it is a very wide topic.